A Casebook
For English Teachers

A Casebook
For English Teachers
Dilemmas and Decisions

Robert C. Small, Jr.
Virginia Tech

Joseph E. Strzepek
University of Virginia

Wadsworth Publishing Company
Belmont, California
A Division of Wadsworth, Inc.

In memory of
Richard Andrew Meade

Education Editor: Suzanna Brabant
Editorial Associate: Cynthia Haus
Designer: Julia Scannell
Cover: Mark McGeoch

Printed in the United States of America   49

1 2 3 4 5 6 7 8 9 10 — — 92 91 90 89 88

ISBN 0-534-08754-X

About the Authors

Robert Small is Professor of English Education at Virginia Tech, where he teaches courses in literature for adolescents and English language arts methods. His degrees are from the University of Virginia, a bachelor's and master's in English and a doctorate in English Education. His publications include *Literature for Adolescents: Selection and Use, Books for You,* and articles in *English Education, English Journal,* and the *ALAN Review.* He has been president of the Adolescent Literature Assembly of the National Council of Teachers of English and chair of NCTE's nominating committee. He is currently co-editor of the *Virginia English Bulletin.*

Joseph Strzepek is Associate Professor of English Education in the Curry School of Education at the University of Virginia. He directs the Central Virginia Writing Project and co-directs the University's Young Writers Summer Workshop, which attracts talented teen-aged poets, journalists, fiction writers, scriptwriters, and songwriters from across the country. He earned a bachelor's degree from Hamilton College, a master's from Harvard University, and a doctorate from Stanford University. He has written for *Four Psychologies Applied to Education, Observation Methods in the Classroom,* the *Virginia English Bulletin,* and *Focus: Teaching English Language Arts.*

Contents

Preface for Students

The recent report of the Task Force on Teaching as a Profession of the Carnegie Forum on Education and the Economy, *A Nation Prepared: Teachers for the 21st Century,* recognizes the value of the case method in teacher education. The report states that an

> ...approach to instruction that should be incorporated into the design of the post-graduate programs is the case method, well developed in law and business, but almost unknown in teaching instruction. Teaching "cases" illustrating a great variety of teaching problems should be developed as a major focus of instruction. (p. 76)

Educators at all levels have rediscovered the fact that an effective teacher is an inquiring teacher. Effective teaching is clearly not the following of a formula by a technician. As a successful teacher you must be both a clinician and a researcher. You must analyze a situation—deal with plagiarism, for instance, or design a poetry unit—draw on resources, develop a solution, implement the solution, examine the results, and make revisions in the strategy or discard it and begin again. Improvement—not absolute success or failure—and discovery are hallmarks of effective teaching. They are also the bases of the case approach to the teaching of English found in this text.

Contained within this book are thirty-three teaching situations or cases drawn from the thousands faced by English teachers every year. In some variation, each has happened more than once to most English teachers. They are based on our own experiences and have been selected because they are representative of the situations in which English teachers make the decisions that control the form that their subject takes in the real world of the school.

The Planning Notebook

This casebook introduces you to the pattern of a planning notebook. Situations are presented; you are asked to analyze them, look for help in deciding what to do, consider the merits of various alternatives, and decide what you would do and why.

Many states have begun to require new teachers to demonstrate on certification exams the ability to write out lesson and unit plans supported by detailed rationales. Student teachers, supervisors, and cooperating teachers have long required such planning and documentation, as have principals and department chairs reviewing teachers facing a tenure review. Personnel specialists often begin interviewing teacher candidates with the questions, "What would you do if...?" and, "Why would you do that?"

It is important, then, that you actually come to look upon this text as your planning workbook. Consequently, the text is designed so that you can write your analyses and your solutions to situations on the pages of the text itself rather than in course notebooks. In this way, you will develop the practice of keeping such a planning book as you move through student teaching into the profession.

Discipline Problems and Teaching Problems

Everyday, English teachers face a variety of challenging problems. Many of these problems spring solely or largely from situations that are beyond the class but that affect what goes on there—students' personal problems, national events, or the weather, for example. More often, however, classroom problems arise from an interaction of the private, the institutional, and the academic. It is one of the basic principles of this book that you will discover best how to deal with the problems of classroom management in the context of the goals, materials, and teaching strategies that form the English language arts.

What is being taught and the way it is being taught influence and are influenced by the attitudes and actions of the students. Equally true, it seems to us, is that improvement in students' attitudes and actions may more often be brought about by changes in the curriculum and the methods of teaching than by any other means within the teacher's control. Therefore, this text gives you the opportunity to deal with such content-related behavior problems within the context of the English class.

Content Problems

An equally large set of problems that confront English teachers relates to what you teach. Prospective teachers of English are usually adequately prepared in the content of their subject—or, at least, better prepared in that content than in what to do with it. The rigor of the undergraduate major does not seem to be a problem so much as the fact that much of what is, or might be, taught in junior and senior high school English classes is typically not a part of that major and is, therefore, unfamiliar to the new teacher. Suggestions for change in the English language arts curriculum, in recent years, have come so rapidly that most experienced teachers also find themselves asked to teach much that is unfamiliar. Also limiting is the prospective teachers' lack of experience in selecting, from all that they know and all that they know how to find, the right pieces of the subject called English for their particular students, the situation, and the goals of the school.

Therefore, many of the cases presented here are designed to give you practice in making such selections. In some of the cases—as in the matter of literature for adolescents—you may find that you are not familiar enough with the subject to be able to make selections. Under those circumstances, the case is designed to point you in the direction of the knowledge that you may lack.

Instructional Problems

Finally, beginning teachers understandably lack the skills needed to design effectively what educators sometimes call "activities" or "strategies." "How do I teach it?" is the plaintive question asked frequently by student teachers who have seen themselves fail to produce learning. As the recent report of the Holmes group has pointed out:

> The last five years of reports on high schools present a dismal account of high school teaching. Most of it is dreary. Teaching consists chiefly of either dull lectures or fact-oriented worksheet assignments. Most teachers exhibit no deep grasp of their subjects, nor any passion for them. Their pedagogy is as sadly lacking as their grip on the material. (p. 16)

When one contemplates the great span of years and maturity from the sixth grade to the twelfth, and of abilities and interests within that span, planning activities that will touch the many varieties of students that are present within a class no doubt seems like an impossible task to the beginning teacher. That the task is not hopeless is proved over and over again each day in the classes of thousands of skillful English teachers. It is also shown by the many studies in which teenagers call the study of literature a positive experience and see it as an aid in achieving self-understanding. In order to help prospective and practicing language arts teachers produce similar attitudes in their students, situations presented in this book support the careful design of a variety of types of activities within the specific details of the case.

The Cases

The cases that follow are detailed and, generally, anecdotal. Nevertheless, as will be obvious, they do not contain every possible piece of information that a teacher should know. The cases are, however, dramatic contexts of real problems that English teachers face regularly. You are asked to read the description of the situation and answer briefly several guide questions that, without providing the solutions themselves, direct your attention to important aspects of the decisions the teacher must make. To help you prepare to work out a solution to the situation, activities are suggested to help you analyze the case and prepare yourself to deal with it. These activities can be the reading of materials that will begin to fill in the gaps in your knowledge of the subject, if such gaps exist. For example, a reference is given to several articles dealing with social dialects as a part of a situation involving a student's non-standard way of speaking. The preparatory activities may also involve the reading of a type of literature with which you are not familiar.

Several alternative solutions are presented for your consideration. These alternative solutions are ones that, in our opinion, practicing English teachers might sometimes follow. They are not necessarily viable solutions, however. In fact, "solutions" that we feel are usually to be avoided have purposely been included to give the reader a chance to react to all types of teaching methods.

When these preliminary activities are complete, you are asked to deal with the case in a way that seems to you to have potential for success and to defend your solution to the situation. Finally, each case ends with a suggested activity called "One More Thing You Might Do" that is designed to help you re-think and consolidate the insights that you have gained.

These cases are planned to help you become a student of teaching. As the recently published National Council of Teachers of English *Guidelines for the Preparation of Teachers of English Language Arts* explained:

> ...they [prospective teachers] need to explore extensively the strategies that are likely to be most successful in teaching various aspects of their subject. They should be encouraged, therefore, to analyze the instruction they receive and observe, asking themselves such questions as "Why is it being done?" "Did it work?" "Why did it work?" "How does it work?"...
>
> Consideration of the nature of effective teaching will be intensive in English language arts methods courses and should also occur in English courses, as students seek to discover patterns and rationales underlying instruction. In addition, prospective teachers need to explore the nature of effective instruction as they deal with learning theory, curriculum, child psychology, and adolescent psychology. Also, they need to develop skill in critically assessing instructional materials such as textbooks and audiovisual materials. Finally, prospective teachers should examine critically the evaluation techniques they experience and observe. (p. 19)

The structure of these cases also follows the generally accepted stages of the writing process, that is, pre-writing, writing, and revision. You are asked, as pre-planning activities, to (a) read the account of the situation, (b) ask yourself several open-ended questions related to the case, (c) carry out some activities related to the case, and (d) consider various possible solutions and note your reactions. Once the pre-planning is complete, you are asked to write your own solution to the situation. In an activity akin to revision, you are asked, separate from the statement of a solution, to provide your justification for that solution. Finally, as a spur to further revision of the plan, you are asked to carry out one final activity.

We have chosen this structure because we have accepted the view that writing is an especially effective way of learning. As Wolfe and Reising say in *Writing for Learning in the Content Areas,* "By writing and re-writing we discover what we know and what we do not know, and we invent new meanings that often startle us" (p. 1). It has become increasingly clear that writing, in addition to its own value as a means of knowing, also is a valuable prelude to discussing.

Preface for Instructors

The cases in this book have been carefully designed to present a full and comprehensive examination of the teaching of English language arts. The teaching of literature, language, and composition is explored, as is evaluation, censorship, materials selection, grouping, and a host of other aspects of the teaching of English. The pre-discussion and follow-up readings and activities may, if the instructor of an English language arts methods class wishes, serve to structure the course. This text may, in other words, serve as a "methods text" for an activity and discussion-centered course. At the same time, this book of cases may serve as a supplement to one of the traditional methods textbooks dealing with the English language arts.

The cases are also planned in such a way that they may serve as an introduction to class discussions exploring questions of what should be done and why it should be done. They may also serve the same purpose in a class organized around small-group discussions. In addition, they may be carried out on an individualized basis, with the descriptions of solutions and the statements of justification presented to the instructor of the class, to other students on a review panel, or to an experienced teacher serving as a respondent. In fact, an instructor of an English language arts methods class will probably want to mix these approaches to provide a variety of strategies for learning.

Finally, when students have completed these activities, they will profit from an opportunity to experience some of them in vivid fashion by role playing. Although every situation will not necessarily be acted out by every student, many of the cases presented here can serve as the bases for valuable improvisations. Role playing has its limits, as does any instructional method; but, given realistic situations, few other devices can serve as well to explore teaching.

Arrangement

The cases in this text are arranged in an order in which they might well be expected to happen during a school year. Thus, although they involve differing grade and ability levels, curriculum organizations, and student and teacher personalities, they give an overall picture of an extended period of teaching English. By dealing with them in the way a teacher must as the class period, the school day, and the school year unfold, prospective teachers can come to sense what the reality of teaching English language arts is.

As they present their ideas to other students in class discussions and in small groups, students will test the validity of their ideas and discover (and perhaps learn to live with) the unsureness inherent in any educational decision. At the same time, they will discover how other teachers might react to the situation, critically examine those reactions, and expand the choices open to them, all with the feeling that they are living through a part of an actual school year.

References

Throughout the cases, we have directed the reader's attention to many books and articles. Each of these references has been selected with two purposes in mind: (a) to provide the reader with assistance in thinking about and developing a response to the case and (b) to introduce the reader to a wide variety of materials in the field of English language arts education. In some cases, the reader is asked to read and respond to an article or a chapter from a book. In others, we have used the term "examine" to suggest that a familiarity with the work will be helpful in working out the case and in dealing later with actual classroom situations. We have tried, therefore, to include references to many books, articles, and journals and to include references to as many as possible of the leaders in the field and their works. Materials referred to in the cases are collected at the end of this volume in a comprehensive bibliography.

Acknowledgements

Before his death in 1983, Richard Meade had been a professor of English Education at the University of Virginia for 48 years. Our mentor and friend, he was one of the founders of the professional education of English teachers. He encouraged the early drafts of this casebook, and we are sure he is smiling at its publication.

We appreciate the invaluable help Patricia Kelly gave us by testing our cases with her pre-service English teachers at Virginia Tech. Stephen Koziol of the University of Pittsburgh read and critiqued two drafts of our manuscript and recommended it to our original editor at Wadsworth, Stephanie Surfus. Her enthusiasm and guidance led us through contracts, successful reviews and revisions, and, happily, publication. Bless you, Pat, Steve, and Stephanie.

For reading our text and offering many useful suggestions, we thank John Bushman of Kansas University, Ruth Cline of the University of Colorado, Carol Pope of the University of Houston at Parkside, and Alice Denham of Texas Tech University. For leading us through the final stages of publication at Wadsworth, we are indebted to our current editor, Suzanna Brabant, and our production editor, Hal Humphrey. For helping us prepare the manuscript, we thank David Starkey of the Virginia Tech College of Education word processing center.

We especially thank our students at our universities for teaching us again what we first learned as high school English teachers: that the best teacher educators are students. We thank them for being so honest and expressive about their dilemmas and decisions.

CASE 1

The Immoral Book

For several months, you've been struggling to find pieces of literature that will interest your third-period sophomore English class. You've had a bit of success with a couple of sports poems, but most of the selections from the literature book haven't interested the student. Also, you've wanted them to read a novel in order to try something longer than a poem or short story. The one in the book, however, *A Tale of Two Cities*, is clearly not for them.

While searching for a novel they might like, you came across an article that recommended Salinger's *The Catcher in the Rye*. You remembered well the first time you'd read *Catcher* and how strong the impact had been on you. The book struck you as appropriate for your third-period students, many of whom seem to you not too different from Holden Caulfield. You were surprised and pleased to find a class set gathering dust in the book room. So you dusted them off and carried them back to your classroom.

Since deciding to teach it, you've given a good deal of thought to how to approach the novel. You've carefully prepared a series of what seem to you to be especially imaginative activities to prepare your students for the first-person autobiographical point of view and for dealing with Holden's various opinions about life and people. The students have spent the last several days writing their own views about people and life in their journals. They've also been listening to and recording the speech of their friends and other people they overhear talking in the cafeteria and locker room, trying to get down on paper how real people speak.

When the day to give out the copies of the book at last arrives, you are optimistic. The students act as if they have enjoyed and profited from the work they have been doing to prepare for reading *Catcher*, and they express an interest in the book itself, the first real interest in a work of literature you've seen from them this year. Those students who have heard of it previously have apparently heard good things about it: "My brother told me about this book," one boy says. "He said it was real good, just like real people."

You talk with them a little bit about the way the story is told, and you drop the term "first-person point of view" into the conversation but don't make an issue of it. Then you read the first page of the novel aloud, make the first reading assignment, and give the students the last half of the period to start their reading. For once, everyone reads, and there are no disturbances. When the bell rings, you have a strong feeling that you've come up with a winner.

That afternoon, as you are preparing to leave school, Mary Wilson, a small, dark-haired, quiet girl from that class, asks to speak with you. Hesitantly, she explains that she doesn't want to read the book because it's "dirty." She tells you that she can't take the book home because her parents wouldn't want her to be reading it. "They wouldn't let a dirty book like that in the house," she says, almost in tears, and she goes on to say that she's sure the parents of the other students wouldn't want their children reading it either. Then she lays her copy of *Catcher* on your desk and looks at you.

Dismayed and -- although you'd heard that *Catcher* had been the cause of some problems in the past in other communities -- unprepared, you ask yourself, "What do I do now?"

A Few Questions You Might Ask Yourself

1. What is there in the novel which a student might object to?

2. Should you attempt to judge the sincerity and merit of such objections? If so, how?

3. If you try to get Mary to read the book and participate in the class, what are the possible results? Which are most probable?

4. If, on the other hand, you yield to her request, what are the possible results? Which are most probable?

5. From what she says, can you be sure how her parents will feel about the novel?

omit

Some Things For You To Do Next

1. Reread Salinger's novel, carefully noting potentially offensive passages.

2. Read some of these passages to your non-English major friends and get their reactions.

3. Contact the chair of the English Department in a local high school. Find out (a) if he/she has had any recent problems with students or parents objecting to literature being taught in the school, and (b) what he/she does to prepare for such problems and to handle them when they arise.

What Do You Think Of Doing The Following?

Don't leave space just type consecutively

1. Telling Mary not to be foolish, the book is a classic of modern American literature, and she'll have to do the assignments just like everyone else.

2. Talking about the book with Mary and seeing how serious her objections are. If she persists, helping her find something else to read.

3. Telling her that you will go through the book and list the numbers of the pages which she should skip in order to avoid offensive material.

4. Asking her to wait until the next day. Then getting a reaction to the book from the other members of the class. If others object, turning the class into an independent reading lesson.

5. Asking Mary to do an extra-credit assignment dealing with the origins of the offensive words.

Now, Write A Description Of How You Would Handle Mary's Objection

Explain Why You Would Do That

One More Thing You Might Do

Read one of the following:

Edward Jenkinson. "Protecting Holden Caulfield and His Friends from the
    Censors," *English Journal*, January, 1985, pp. 26-33.

Wayne Booth. "Censorship and the Values of Fiction," *English Journal*, March,
    1964, pp. 155-164.

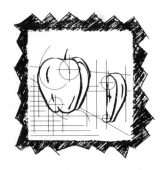

Dialect Prejudice

When you arrive at school the first morning of the second semester, the principal tells you that you have a new student in your second-period, ninth-grade class. His name is Junior Smith, until now a resident of the Appalachian part of the state, where his father was a seasonal laborer. In class you notice that Junior is uncomfortable and sensitive to the stares he and his patched overalls are receiving.

When you introduce Junior to the class and ask him a few friendly questions about his former home, his answers provoke giggles and sarcastic comments:

"Boy, do you talk funny. Where'd you learn to talk like that?" says Hugh Middleton. Manuel Rameriz, however, tells Hugh to shut up and leave Junior alone.

You stop the class, staring coldly until there is silence. Just then a fire drill buzzer rings. "Saved by the bell," you say to yourself as you usher the students out.

When the fire drill is over, it is time for the third period. As you begin that class, you wonder what will you do tomorrow in your second-period class.

Your grammar and composition textbooks discuss the importance of stressing the use of "standard" or "edited" American English in formal writing and are full of examples of standard and nonstandard usage items that frequently appear on standardized tests. The same text stresses the importance of tolerating, in fact, of appreciating, the rich variety of regional accents and dialects in our pluralistic nation.

Your school is a large, comprehensive suburban high school in which students are tracked by academic ability. Your second-period class is composed of average or "general" students, some of whom will go to college and some directly to the workforce. Your state is torn between a rabid "English is America's language" faction and an ever-growing population of non-English speaking minorities who demand the right to be taught in their own languages. You understand all that, but none of it helps. What will you do to prepare for your second-period class tomorrow?

A Few Questions You Might Ask Yourself

1. What are the causes of dialect prejudice? How should you deal with it?

2. Should a student's oral language be corrected to conform to standard American English?

3. What are the relationships among grammar, usage, slang, and regional dialects?

4. How do you feel when adults you meet scatter or become self-consciously mute when they discover you are an English teacher?

5. How do you feel when other adults blame your profession for the decline of English?

Some Things For You To Do Next

1. Read James Sledd's article in the December, 1969 *English Journal*, "Bidialectism: The Linguistics of White Supremacy," pp. 1307-1315, 1329.

2. Listen to the speech of several of your friends. Does the way they use the English language affect the way you think about them? If so, how?

3. Read Chapter 4: "Common Errors" (pp. 90-159) in Mina Shawnessy's *Errors and Expectations* (Oxford University Press, 1977), and consider the problem of diagnosing the origins of so-called errors in usage.

What Do You Think Of Doing The Following?

1. Asking the students to listen for different dialects on TV and radio. Playing tapes and records demonstrating different dialects in the U.S.

2. Asking the students to notice the effects of dialects, especially ones which occur in literature, the media, and real life.

3. Preparing optional remedial oral practice drills in standard English for those
    students who wish to improve their ability to speak the standard dialect.

4. Inviting a dialectologist from a nearby university who as part of his/her
    presentation can wow the students by identifying exactly where a speaker
    comes from.

5. Reminding students that in a democracy, linguistic diversity should not only
    be tolerated but valued, especially in speech. Tell them, however, that writing
    is another story, because in writing we should use standard English in order
    to succeed academically and economically.

**Now, Write What You Would Do To Prepare To Meet Your Class
Tomorrow**

Explain Why You Would Do That

One More Thing To Do

Read:

"A Proposed Position Statement: Students' Right to Their Own Language,"
Conference on College Composition and Communication, Spring 1974, pp.
1-19.

Then state your own position on student language.

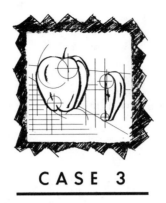

CASE 3

Thinking for Yourself

During a unit on *Macbeth*, you observe that your class is unusually susceptible to arguments based on authority and emotion rather than reason and the logic of evidence. Few dare to argue with Gloria Smythe, your most sarcastic student, and even fewer venture to differ with Rick "Rambo" Rogers whenever you ask the class to question each other's interpretations. You decide to prepare a class designed to startle them into thinking more critically. As the class begins, you list on the blackboard the following names: Eve, Lucrezia Borgia, Delilah, the Sirens, Wicked Witch of Oz, Lizzy Borden, hurricanes Agnes and Camille, Jezebel, Pandora, Helen of Troy, Madame Defarge, and Lady Macbeth.

The class starts buzzing when they see the list. First, you ask them to identify each name on the list, and next you ask what the list seems to add up to. With very little prodding, the statement, "Women are the root of all evil," is made, and you write that on the board. There are cries of objection from a few girls; one is even brave enough to call you a "chauvinist" but not quite brave enough to add "pig." Most of the girls, however, sit passively stunned, while their "gentlemen" classmates smile or nod in agreement with the statement.

When you then apply the principle to *Macbeth*, you say, "Logically, then it follows that Lady Macbeth is the sole cause of Macbeth's tragic downfall, because she put him up to murdering Duncan. He would have remained happy as Thane of Cawdor without her pressure to climb the social ladder." This statement provokes a few more murmured female objections but not many more.

So far so good, but where do you take the lesson from here?

A Few Questions You Might Ask Yourself

1. How could you let your students know they are allowed to differ with you without fear of penalty?

2. What kinds of training do you think your students would have had before their junior year in logic, argumentation, propaganda analysis, and debate techniques?

3. How could you get your students to argue back without *telling* them exactly what is wrong with your argument?

Some Things You Might Do Next

1. Try to disprove or verify your own arguments by examining (a) the text of *Macbeth*, (there are a number of lines which indicate Macbeth himself was ambitious and might well have killed Duncan eventually without Lady Macbeth's insistence); (b) the universe of female literary and historical figures, (a long list of good women could be constructed); and (c) the universe of male figures, (a lengthy list of male villains could be generated).

2.   Consider how one proves or disproves anything, and consider the difference between being right and winning an argument.

3.   Examine the NCTE publications for students on critical thinking: Dan Kirby and Carol Kuykendall, *Thinking Through Language, Book One*, and B. D. Stanford and Gene Stanford, *Thinking Through Language, Book Two* (NCTE, 1985).

What Do You Think Of Doing The Following?

1.   Explaining to the students the fallacies in your argument and showing them how it was an example of "card stacking" and faulty generalization from a sample selected with a bias.

2.   Asking the class to discuss the difference between arguments about moral or normative questions and questions of fact; that is, the fact that whether or not ends justify means is a different order question from whether one character or another is the killer.

3.   Having the class read from recent publications related to the Women's Liberation Movement and staging a debate on the adoption of the Equal Rights Amendment.

4. Reading the class James Thurber's "The Macbeth Murder Mystery," a satirical story about a woman so addicted to the surprising solutions of the "whodunit" genre of mystery stories that she was convinced that Macduff killed Duncan. It is published in *My World and Welcome To It* and *The Thurber Carnival.*

Write A Plan For The Rest Of The Lesson

Explain Why You Would Do That

One More Thing You Might Do

Take a look at S. I. Hayakawa's *Language in Thought and Action* (Harcourt Brace Jovanovich, 1972), especially pp. 54-68.

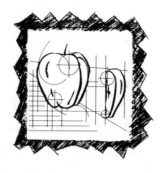

CASE 4

Ethnic Literature or Just Literature?

At the English Department meeting on Wednesday afternoon, a delegation of three black students from one of your classes -- Susan, Patty, and Jim -- presents a petition signed by thirty-five students. The petition asks that a course in Black Literature be offered as an elective in place of the regular English courses. These students point out that many black authors are still not included in the textbook and that those that are included are represented by, at most, one or two poems, often neither their best nor their most angry.

They explain calmly that many other schools in the area offer Black Literature courses. They end their presentation by listing the names of black authors that they would like to study in more depth than is possible in the required English classes.

Very conscious that you are a white teacher, you listen carefully.

The students are polite and clearly well prepared. And they are politely received. But, when they have left, an intradepartmental argument begins to rage.

Henry Jackson, whose approach to everything, especially education, is very conservative, maintains loudly that literature is literature. "I, for one, am opposed to teaching Black Literature or White Literature. If it's worth teaching, I'll teach it."

Susan Gibson, the newest member of the department, stands up and, her voice shaking, points out sarcastically, "All of you teach *White Literature* since almost nothing but white authors are in our textbooks." Her face burning, she sits down abruptly.

"That's right," comments Ruth Logan, who prides herself on her progressive views. "Langston Hughes is a better poet than Longfellow, but he gets only a poem or two when Longfellow gets a dozen. Besides," she continues, "we teach American Literature, Romantic Literature, Elizabethan Literature. Why not Black Literature?" With a sneer at Henry Jackson, she folds her arms and tosses her head back.

Pat Henderson, usually a voice of reason, tries to maintain that black authors should be taught, but as a part of the regular course. "Not in a separate class," she pleads. "That would be a ghetto class." She ends her statement by offering to share her collection of works by minority authors with anyone who wants them.

As the argument rages around you, you remember the boredom that seemed to develop in your black students when you moved from that composition unit you'd worked up in the summer writing project to the poetry unit. The black students had written enthusiastically about their lives as students -- and sometimes as black students. But the poetry had left them cold.

Reviewing the poets included in the textbook, you realize that they are mostly white. You wonder whether that fact could be the cause of the black students' lack of interest. You ask yourself, do black students really want to read mostly black writers? Should white students study black authors as *black* authors or just as authors? How should black students approach black authors? And white authors, for that matter?

And, do you know enough about Black Literature to teach it? Should it be a separate class? Should the teacher be black? What a muddle!

You awake from your reverie to hear Ruth say, "As a matter of fact, it shouldn't be just Black Literature we teach. It should be Native American Literature, Chicano Literature..."

"And Women's Literature," Susan adds. "Why not that?"

What in the world is the answer? Ethnic Literature? Gender Literature? Or just Literature?

A Few Questions You Might Ask Yourself

1. Why do you think black, Indian, Chicano, etc., writers have often been left out of most high school literature texts? How well represented are they now?

2. Were the black students asking for Black Literature for themselves or for all students, black, other minorities, and white?

3. Is grouping writers of an ethnic minority for study comparable to the grouping involved in units in the romantic writers or a course in American Literature? What part should a consideration of the characteristics of the author play in the study of literature in high school? Should a teacher do anything different when teaching a work of Black Literature than when teaching any work of literature?

4. How much do you know about ethnic writers? How many have you read?

5. Are there any special problems which might arise in teaching ethnic literature? In teaching a specific ethnic work?

6. And what about women writers? How well represented are they?

Some Things For You To Do Next

1. Examine several different standard high school literature books. What selections by black authors are represented? Chicano authors? American Indian authors? Other ethnic authors? Women authors? Can you recognize such authors?

2. Examine an anthology of minority writers such as the following and ask yourself how many of the authors and works you recognize, how many you have studied, how good they are by objective critical standards:
    A. Chapman, ed., *Black Voices* (New American Library, 1968) or Dorothy Strickland, ed., *Listen Children* (Bantam, 1982).

3. Examine *Black Literature for High School Students* by Barbara Dodds Stanford and Karina Amin (NCTE, 1978).

What Do You Think Of Doing The Following?

1. Using one of several anthologies of Black Literature which are designed for high school students to prepare a unit in "The Black Experience" for later in the year.

2. Including several poems by ethnic and women writers in the unit now under way and making a note to supplement the literature in the next units with minority and women writers as you develop those units.

3. Determining that the black students will learn to see the greatness and universality of the writers included in the literature anthology.

4. Relegating the study of black, ethnic, and women's literature to individual or special projects for those who are interested.

5. Planning an annual Ethnic Studies Week as a program to educate the uninformed, to stimulate ethnic pride, and to relieve the pressure being brought by student activists.

6. Petition the principal to support an ad hoc curriculum committee composed of teachers, students, and parents to study the issue during the summer and make specific recommendations for course and curriculum revisions.

Now, Write A Plan For Your Department's Approach To Minority And Women Writers

Explain Why You Would Do That

One More Thing You Might Do

Interview a high school teacher of a Black Literature class and one who teaches Black writers as part of a general literature class. Try to find out their views on this question. Can you find a course or unit in other ethnic minority writers being taught? A course in women writers? Try to find out how blacks, other ethnic groups, and women are studied as cultures and as individuals in other subject areas, especially social studies.

CASE 5

Writing: Creative, Practical, or Is There Any Difference?

Although your school had recently instituted an elective course in creative writing, you have continued to devote a good deal of time in your regular English classes to the writing of descriptions, narratives, plays, poems and stories because you strongly believe that all students should have an opportunity to carry out what is usually called "creative writing," not just the few who have the time and inclination to take an elective course. You have assigned an occasional formal essay, but you haven't lost your belief that students enjoy and personally benefit more from freer, more informal, more purely creative types of writing. Consequently, you have had the students keep "writer's notebooks"; and, as much as possible, you have avoided the traditional English teacher role of marking and grading.

At Back to School Night, when the parents of your students have been invited to meet their children's teachers, see the school, and hear about what's going on in the various classes their children are taking, you expressed your ideas about composition. You were shocked when many of the parents raised questions about your ideas.

"My son isn't going to be a poet," one father said. "He needs to be able to fill out an application for a job and write reports to his boss." Another father asked, "How many poems and short stories will my daughter have to write in college? I don't remember writing any myself."

Obviously, many of the parents wanted their children to receive training in practical writing. They saw "creative writing" as a frill and nothing more. Yet you want writing to be a means that students can use now and later to express and clarify for themselves their thoughts, ideas, and feelings. On the other hand, you don't want them to fail in college or lose jobs because they can't handle the practical aspects of writing. You feel an obligation to their parents, but you know that the skills learned in creative writing will help the students with practical writing.

The next day in class, therefore, you ask the students how they feel about the kind of writing they have been doing this year. The reaction is mixed. Several students raise the same points that the parents had the night before. In addition, you discover that many students feel that being asked to write poems and stories is somehow unfair. As Susan puts it, "It takes a special talent to do that sort of thing. That's why there are only a few great writers. Well, I don't have that sort of talent, and I don't see why I have to keep on writing bad poems and stories. It's frustrating to spend all that time and know that you're going to end up with something no one will want to read, not even yourself."

Other students raise the question of grades. It's clear that they want more of their work graded -- as one says, "If I'm going to write it, I want you to grade it." And a couple of students ask you just how anyone can grade a poem or a story. You understand, of course, that, in a nice way, they are questioning your ability to judge their creative work.

Troubled by their reaction -- especially since you thought they would tell you that creative writing was more rewarding and more fun than writing dull essays -- you realize that you need to offer a more persuasive argument for the importance of creative writing or change to assigning and grading essays and research papers.

A Few Questions You Might Ask Yourself

1. How much writing do most adults do? What kinds of writing do they do most frequently? What skills do these kinds of writing require?

2. How clear a distinction is there between "creative" and other types of writing? How different are the skills needed for each?

3. Can so-called "creative" forms of writing play a valuable part in the lives of those who do not write professionally or even very well?

4. Can "creative" writing be taught? If so, in what sense and how?

Some Things For You To Do Next

1. Examine Kenneth Koch's *Rose, Where Did You Get That Red?* (Random House, 1973). Try writing a poem following one of his models or poetry ideas.

2. Survey a number of your friends who are not professional writers. Try to find out whether or not they have recently written anything that might be called "creative."

3. Ask a friend to write poems for you for the next day. Consider his/her reactions and the nature of the products.

4. Examine the writing in a high school literary magazine, especially the winning writing in a contest such as the Scholastic competition, which is published each year. Realizing that this is among the very best of high school writing, what conclusions can you draw?

What Do You Think Of Doing The Following?

1. Recommending that your students take the elective creative writing class and then concentrating in your classes during the next several units on various forms of expository, report, and technical writing.

2. Organizing the curriculum so that the younger students -- grades seven through nine or ten -- concentrate on creative writing and the juniors and seniors work mostly on expository writing.

3. Demonstrating to the class how practice in organizing and dramatizing fictional narratives and poetry can help them write more effective reports and essays.

4. Inviting a local writer to lead a Poet-in-the-School unit for your students.

5. Making an anthology of the best creative writing done by your students and sending it to their parents.

Now, What Would You Do About Creative Writing?

Write Your Argument To Justify That Approach

One More Thing You Might Do

Examine the following:

Peter Stillman, *Writing Your Way* (Boyton/Cook, 1984).

CASE 6

Killing *Caesar*

With high hopes, you plunge your tenth-grade class into a five-week unit on Shakespeare's *Julius Caesar*. You begin by assigning reports on Shakespeare's life, times, and stage, showing movies on Elizabethan England, and playing records on Elizabethan music and lyrics. You even bring in Ms. Gaston, the Latin teacher, to team teach a lesson on Caesar as a historical figure.

Then comes the first class discussion and in-class reading of *Caesar*. You set the scene for the class and begin by reading the opening lines yourself, explicating and asking questions as you read. Next you direct the last half of the scene to be read aloud by students who volunteer to take specific parts.

The students read haltingly and reverently as if they were leading devotions. You assign the class the rest of Act I for the next day's assignment. The following day the students read out loud at their desks again; the class is restless but struggles dutifully with the arguments of the conspirators Cassius and Brutus. By the end of the period, however, students are groaning, asking who cares about the Romans anyhow?

To your dismay, the rest of the week gets worse.

"We can't pronounce these words, and we don't know what they mean," says a class spokesperson. "Why can't you show us a video or movie first the way our teacher did last year when we read *Merchant of Venice?*"

You had planned to show the Marlon Brando movie of *Julius Caesar* at the end of the unit as a culminating experience, rather than now. Should you follow your original plan or show the film now? What else can you do to help your students with *Caesar?*

A Few Questions You Might Ask Yourself

1. Why teach *Julius Caesar* to tenth graders? What kinds of knowledge, skills, and attitudes might or should you be trying to develop in this unit? Could another, more contemporary play generate those learnings more easily than *Caesar?*

2. What other instructional patterns for teaching a play could you choose? Is it too late to change to another?

3. What kind of dramatic backgrounds do you think the students would have? Would they have seen or acted in plays? How would they have been taught plays in previous years?

Something You Might Do Next

1. Make a list of the objectives of a unit on *Julius Caesar*. Which do you think are the most important? Consider how you would evaluate the students' progress.

2. Identify three recent plays you might use with high school students. Consider the advantages of these plays when compared to *Caesar*. What would you lose by substituting one of these plays for *Caesar*?

3. Reread *Julius Caesar* and select the key themes and passages that you might ask a tenth-grade class to study.

4. Read Larry Crapse's argument for teaching *Caesar* in "A Symposium on Pre-1900 Classics Worth Teaching," *English Journal*, March, 1983, pp. 51-52.

What Do You Think Of Doing The Following?

1. Assigning parts ahead of time and giving daily grades for oral reading and discussion.

2. Substituting a viewing and study of the Brando movie for a reading of the play.

3. Selecting *Caesar* records to be played as the class follows along in the playbooks.

4. Assigning the rest of the play to be read immediately, so that the play could be discussed as a whole rather than scene by scene, and cutting the unit length to three weeks.

5. Dropping *Caesar* and substituting *Raisin in the Sun.*

6. Taking the class to the auditorium where they can read the play on stage.

7. Assigning poor readers to make costumes and props for the good readers who will memorize Act III for presentation for a parents' night performance.

Now, Write What You Would Do With The Rest Of Julius Caesar

Explain Why You Would Do That

One More Thing You Might Do

Read the conclusions of James Hoetker's study on teaching drama, *Students as Audiences: An Experimental Study of the Relationship Between Classroom Study of Drama and Attendance at the Theatre* (NCTE Report No. 11, 1971).

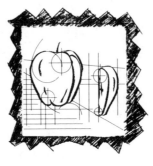

CASE 7

Poetry Is Boring

It seemed like such a good unit. Although you knew that junior high school students weren't generally thought to like poetry, you were sure that, with the proper approach, they could be brought to enjoy and appreciate poetry for its richness of language and emotion and its thought-provoking qualities. Following several weeks of careful planning, you came up with what you thought was a good unit. After having the class read nursery rhymes, several simple poems like "Casey at the Bat" and "The Cremation of Sam McGee," and a few poetic prose passages, you started with the question, "What is poetry?"

Although the students didn't seem very interested in the answer to the question, they did discuss why they didn't like poetry, whatever it was. At the end of the first day, therefore, you felt pleased about the participation. The next day, you played a recording of "The Bells" while the students listened -- and, unfortunately, laughed -- and then talked about the way Poe used the sounds of the words to create the sense of different kind of bells. "It doesn't say anything" and "It doesn't make sense" seemed to be the consensus. Seeing a lack of interest developing, you assigned "The Rime of the Ancient Mariner" for homework and gave the students the last fifteen minutes to start reading. They were soon whispering, looking out the window, and sleeping. The bell rang before you could decide what to do.

The next day, you began the study of the poem by asking whether the students believed in ghosts. A fairly lively discussion followed; but, when you turned their attention to the supernatural in "The Ancient Mariner," interest flagged. Despite your efforts to get the students to see how vivid Coleridge's images are and how musical his language is, the students continued to show lack of interest and to complain that it didn't make sense. Several more days of this poem produced little enthusiasm, and the next three poems you studied provoked sighs and complaints. The students seemed to be saying, "We told you poetry is boring. See!"

Now as you review the rest of your unit -- a dozen more poems; lessons on rhyme, figures of speech, and rhythm patterns; a study of several American poets -- you are worried. Each day the students are less interested in the reading of poetry; and, at best, their interest has been more in the discussion of ghosts and prejudice and other topics related to the poems than in the poems themselves. How can students be brought to like poetry? You feel sure you haven't found the answer.

A Few Questions You Might Ask Yourself

1. What is poetry? How many people like it? Why do they? Do you? Why do people dislike it?

2. When do people read poetry? How do they read it? How do they pick poems to read?

3. What is there about adolescents that would make them like poems? What would make them dislike them? Is there any kind of poetry that many teenagers like?

4. Why should teenagers read poetry?

5. What are teenagers interested in reading about? What approaches to these subjects do they like best? Are there poems about those subjects? Are they written in a way that would appeal to the teenage reader?

Some Things For You To Do Next

1. Reread the poems that these students were asked to study for the unit. Consider what problems of language, etc. they might present to junior high school students. Ask yourself whether or not the subjects and the ways those subjects are treated are likely to interest the students.

2. Read a dozen or more "standard" poems from a high school literature anthology or some other collection. Consider how you felt about the poems. Did you like them all? How many? Did you enjoy reading that many poems at one time?

3. Examine several collections of nontraditional poems such as Lee Bennett Hopkins' *Movements* (Harcourt Brace Jovanovich, 1980) and consider how student might feel about those poems.

4. Discuss poetry with several non-English-major friends. Try to find out how they feel about poetry, why, and what poems they like.

5. Read "The Making of a Poetry Program" by Michael Jones in the *English Journal*, October, 1985, pp. 63-65.

What Do You Think Of Doing The Following?

1. Gathering a large collection of poetry anthologies, instructing the students to browse, then asking each student to find one poem he or she likes and to share

it with the class. Using those poems as the content for the remainder of the poetry unit.

2.   Analyzing several poems in detail to show the students how poets use metaphors, assonance, rhyme, etc. and to teach them how to read poetry.

3.   Giving up on poetry for the time being and hoping that as they grow older and more mature the students will learn to like it.

4.   Establishing a poetry time each week when anyone -- teacher or student -- can bring a poem for the class to look at.

5.   Taking the class to hear a live reading by a poet.

Now, Describe How You Would Teach Poetry

Explain Why You Would Handle It That Way

One More Thing You Might Do

Read one of the following:

Arthea J. S. Reed. "Poetry," *Reaching Adolescents: The Young Adult Book and the School* (Holt, Rinehart and Winston, 1985), pp. 172-180.

Gene Stanford, ed., "Getting Involved in Poetry," *Activating the Passive Student* (NCTE, 1979), pp. 95-121.

Charles R. Duke and Sally A. Jacobsen, eds. *Reading and Writing Poetry: Successful Approaches for the Student and Teacher* (Oryx Press, 1983).

Role Playing

You lead your eleventh-grade class through a discussion of John Knowle's short story "Phineas." The story ends with Gene Forester about to confront his best friend, Phineas, at his house. A few weeks earlier Gene had caused Phineas to fall from a tree and shatter his leg, thereby ruining his future as an athlete. To test your students' understanding of Gene and Phineas's characters, to prepare them to read Knowles' *A Separate Peace*, a novel which further develops the story of Gene and Phineas, and to experiment with dramatic and interpretive techniques, you ask your class to role play what will happen when the door opens and Phineas sees Gene.

You begin by asking the students to imagine what will occur. Then you call on Wade Lowe and Art Bash to "play" Gene and Phineas in front of the class. They face each other awkwardly, then stammer a few lines:

Wade as Gene: "How's your leg, Finny?"

Art as Finny: "O.K. old buddy. Good to see you."

Wade: "When are you coming back to school?"

Art: "In a few weeks."

They continue this way without ever touching the problem of whether Gene will confess his act or whether Phineas realizes what his friend did to him.

You get impatient and ask two other students to take the parts. While all this is going on the class is restless and uncertain. You urge the two new role players to be more dramatic.

Bob as Gene: "I'm sorry you fell, Finny."

Alan as Phineas: "The hell you are! You jounced the limb! Get out of my house!"

With that, Finny (Alan) gets up and pushes Gene (Bob) in the stomach. A fight nearly breaks out, as the rest of the class shouts and encourages the combatants.

You stop the fight and settle the class, but you don't know whether your experiment in role playing has succeeded or failed. What can you do to use what happened in the role playing to help the class with their interpretations of the characters and events in "Phineas" and in *A Separate Peace*?

A Few Questions You Might Ask Yourself

1. What were the reasons for the different students' behaviors? Do you think they have ever been involved in role playing before?

2. How well were the actors and audience prepared to participate in this exercise? Do you think the class had a good understanding of the characters of Gene and Phineas and how they felt in this situation?

3. What kind of responses would you have expected from the role players?

4. Should you try another set of actors after spending some time redirecting the class and prospective players?

Some Things You Might Do Next

1. Consider how Gene and Phineas would feel if, as in the first role playing, they both persisted in denying what had happened on the limb. Then ask yourself how that continual denial might affect both characters and their relationship.

2. Write a description of your students' responses to the second role playing: Phineas denounces Gene, while Gene denies responsibility.

3. Read Fannie R. Shaftel and George Shaftel, *Role Playing for Social Values* (Prentice-Hall, 1967) for instruction on how to lead role playing.

What Do You Think of Doing the Following?

1. Telling your students what actually happens in *A Separate Peace* during this confrontation.

2. Using role playing for studying drama and using traditional discussion methods with literature.

3. Taking a part yourself the next time you use role playing.

4. Breaking the class into small groups or pairs so that everyone gets to participate at once instead of having most of the class be a passive audience.

5. Preparing the audience to participate by giving them things to watch for and critique.

6. Taking the class to see the movie *A Separate Peace*.

Now, Write How You Would Follow Up Your Students' Enactments

Explain Why You Would Do That

More Things You Might Do

Select another piece of literature that you believe students would like and consider how you might use role playing in teaching it.

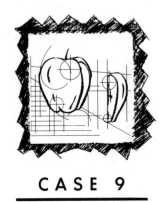

CASE 9

I Never Could Spell

All through college your own inability to spell plagued you. Professors often remarked on your papers about your weak spelling: the kind ones commented but graded you on other matters; less kind professors wrote, "You would have gotten an A- but the spelling, oh dear!" and gave you a C.

Now, as a beginning English teacher, you have sworn to yourself that you will teach your students how to spell. Poor spelling, you are convinced from your own experience, is a practical handicap, whatever else it may or may not be.

At the beginning of the year, therefore, you began a systematic series of spelling lessons. To be sure that you were dealing with the right words, you drew your list of words for tests from an older edition of the grammar-composition book that is still used in the school. You used the older book because the newest edition, the one the school just adopted, doesn't have a list of spelling words. Still, the list in the older edition of the book had many words that you knew your students would have trouble with.

Each Monday you have dictated twenty words, then read out the spellings as the students checked their papers. Next, you have talked briefly about each word, pointing out the problems it might give, asking students to share their difficulties with it, and reviewing what it means. Then, each Friday, you have given a test on those words plus five more that the students had had trouble with on the earlier tests. *Advantage*, *adventure*, and *advice*; *badge*, *baggage*, and *balcony*: you've worked your way though the list.

In addition, you have drawn attention to the spelling words when they appeared in the stories and poems in the literature book; and you've brought in examples and asked the students to bring in examples of the words from the newspaper and from television shows. Also, you've graded carefully the spelling errors on the students' compositions and other written work. All together, you have carried out a comprehensive and intensive spelling program.

As the year has progressed, you have discovered that the grades on the spelling tests are generally fairly good, and that has encouraged you. Indeed, some of the weaker students seem to do best on those tests. But the spelling in the students' written work has remained unchanged and generally poor. Often, the students have misspelled in their compositions words that they had spelled correctly on the weekly tests. More often, they have misspelled certain common words that you had felt were too simple for those tests, words like *their* and *too*.

Trying to make the tests relate to the actual spelling problems of the students, you have begun to bring up in class the words that you find misspelled in their compositions, discuss them, and add them to the tests. Still, their spelling has not improved. You have continued to find *thier* and *occassionally*, *two* for *too* and *here* for *hear*. No amount of weekly review and testing has helped. Perfect spellers like Mary and Susan have continued to get 100% on their tests. Most students have spelled moderately well but often erratically on the tests. And a few poor souls like Jeff and George have continued to be unable to spell correctly even the most common words.

Now, at the end of the first semester, you feel more sympathy for your own English teachers in high school. And you can't help but feel sorry for George, Jeff, and the other weak spellers, since they remind you so much of yourself at that age. Still, that just makes you all the more determined to help them. But how?

A Few Questions You Might Ask Yourself

1. What problems do you yourself have with spelling? Why do you misspell words when you do? How often? What kinds of words give you the most trouble?

2. How often does a misspelled word cause misunderstanding? How often does it distract the reader?

3. Why is spelling according to a standard form considered important? How is the standard form established? How accurate is the spelling of most educated people?

4. To what extent is misspelling a reading problem or a proofreading problem?

Some Things For You To Do Next

1. Examine a spelling list designed for high school use such as those found in most standard grammar-composition books. Consider the usefulness of the words and their difficulty.

2. Select some of the more difficult words from the list and ask several friends to spell them. How well did they do?

3. Discuss spelling with a number of non-English-major friends. How much trouble to they admit having? How important do they feel spelling is? Why?

4. Read the following:

    "Spelling" in *The Teaching of Writing* by John H. Bushman (Charles C. Thomas, 1984), pp. 152-157.

What Do You Think Of Doing The Following?

1. Requiring students to keep a personal spelling lists of words they have problems with or which, because of their interests or future plans, they feel a need to be sure of. Then dividing the class into teams and having the students help each other to practice these words.

2. Dropping the entire subject of spelling as unimportant and impossible to solve.

3. Emphasizing careful proofreading rather than ability to spell extemporaneously and using peer editing groups to catch typos and spelling errors.

4. Urging the students to use dictionaries to find the right word or a synonym they can spell.

5. Showing your chronic misspellers how they can use a programmed proofreader to identify misspellings in texts they type into a word processor.

Now, Describe How You Would Treat Spelling

Explain Why You Would Do That

One More Thing You Might Do

Look up in several dictionaries a number of the more commonly misspelled words,
such as *separate (seperate)*. Are the misspellings present? If so, how are they

labeled? Then examine *Improving Spelling and Vocabulary in the Secondary School* by Richard E. Hodges (NCTE, 1982).

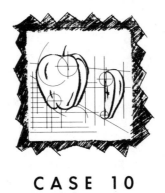

CASE 10

Writing Groups

You have studied how to direct students through the writing process, and you have had experience in writers' workshops and writing groups. You want your students to write frequently, to rough out free writings and first drafts, to revise those drafts, polish, edit, and publish them. You know the best way for you to accomplish this goal is to train your students to comment constructively on each other's papers in small writing groups. You have concluded that small groups, when effective, not only give the students real audiences to write for but also speed up the revision process and improve the quality of the final drafts you eventually grade.

Now that you have your own classes to work with, you decide to begin teaching your students how to comment constructively on other students' papers by putting a paper (unnamed) borrowed from another teacher on the overhead projector and asking your students to write down what they would say to the author of the paper. When you ask several students to read their comments, they range from overly critical to neutral to "it's very good, I like it." None of the comments is specific enough to the text to be useful to the writer, and far too many deal with minor mechanical errors. Margie, one of your weakest spellers, manages to find five misspellings that don't exist. George's most helpful comment is, "It's dumb!"

Your students are obviously not ready to be turned loose on others' papers in small groups. What can you do to get them ready?

A Few Questions You Might Ask Yourself

1. What kinds of comments are useful to you as a writer?

2. Would you rather receive oral or written comments on your writing?

3. What kinds of comments are appropriate for papers and writers at different stages of development? How many comments can young writers effectively process and apply?

4. What kinds of comments are most helpful in improving writing: Descriptive? Interpretive? Evaluative? Reader based? Criterion based?

Some Things You Might Do Next

1. Consider what might happen if you ask students to read one set papers to each other in groups of three to five in order to share them without commenting on them and without apologies, excuses, or explanations by the writer.

2. Read Peter Elbow's explanations of types of feedback in *Writing With Power*, Chapter 5, pp. 237-277 (Oxford University Press, 1981).

3. Comment on a paper you wrote a year or two ago and consider what kinds of comments would be appropriate for the paper if it had been written by a high school student.

4. Decide what role the teacher should play while writing groups are working: participant, observer, or classroom manager.

What Would You Think Of Doing The Following?

1. Making a videotape of a working writing group composed of experienced writers and responders to show to your class.

2. For the first three writing groups, having your students restrict their comments to positive and descriptive or summarizing comments (that is, reflecting back to the writer what parts strike them as most prominent, and restating what they feel is the main idea or effort of the paper).

3. Preparing a handout which assigns the students to specific groups and assigning each to play special roles, for example, timekeeper, describer, interpreter, or evaluator.

4. Having a group of five different students serve as a model workshop group once each week with you as leader and first responder.

5. Restricting workshop groups to the tasks of proofreading and editing so you
    do not have to mark errors when you grade.

Now, Describe How You Can Prepare Your Students To Help Each Other

Identify The Parts Of Your Plan You Feel Most Confident About. Why? Least Confident About? Why?

One More Thing To Do

Read
> Ken Macrorie Ch. 10: "The Helping Circle," in *Writing to Be Read* (Boyton/Cook, 1976), pp. 84-94.

The Unread Story

Since you first saw that it was in the literature book, you had looked forward to teaching Jack London's short story, "To Build a Fire." You remembered enjoying it when you'd read it in an American literature class in high school, and you felt sure the students in your average ninth-grade class would also like it.

You liked it especially because London had exerted such great control over the slow development of the plot and the limited setting. Also you felt confident that London was a person your students would find interesting. His life was adventurous and nonconformist. You were sure that they would identify with that approach to life.

So, on Monday morning, you begin the lesson by telling them about London's life. Following your brief lecture, you assign the story to be read by the students at their desks. They settle down quickly to the reading; and, after a few minutes, you notice that John, who often stares out the window when the class is reading or discussing literature, seems to be reading intently.

Pleased, you look around the class and discover that Sandra, who is usually more interested in boys than school, is also reading quietly. Even more pleased, though a bit surprised, you walk quietly to the side of the room so you can see the expressions on the faces of other students.

London's life had done it, you say to yourself. You knew they'd find him interesting. But, when you look across the room again at Sandra, you discover that she is, in fact, deeply engrossed in a magazine that is hidden behind her textbook, a "true romance" magazine from the look of it. Suspicious, you look more closely at John from your new viewpoint and see what appears to be a hot-rod magazine open on his lap.

Much less pleased now, you tell yourself that they haven't given the story a chance. Yet you have to admit that Sandra probably would not have finished "To Build a Fire," even if she had started it. Perhaps it is your disappointment, but the rest of the students now seem to be bored and restless. Several seem to be merely staring blankly at the pages; and, worse, a number are now looking out the window. There is that subdued noise in the room that, you know by experience, means a lack of interest.

The class discussion that follows confirms your worst fears. Most of the students appear to dislike the story, and the majority seems not to have read very far and not to have understood what they read.

Now, looking back on the class, you have a pretty strong suspicion that most of the other students would have preferred Sandra's romance magazine or John's stories of hot rods. Still, you're determined to do something about your students' apathy.

A Few Questions You Might Ask Yourself

1. What was your purpose in choosing this story? What results did you hope to achieve?

2. Why did you introduce it by talking about Jack London's life? What else might you have done as an introduction?

3. Why do you think John and Sandra chose magazines they did? What is the appeal of such magazines for them?

4. Do you think that there is one best way to teach a short story? Should you have taught the story in the way you have handled previous works of literature with this class?

Some Things For You To Do Next

1. Read "To Build a Fire." Examine its style -- sentence structure, vocabulary, etc. Consider the way it is told, its story line, its characters. Try to imagine what experiences John and Sandra might have had that are similar to the experiences of the main character in the story.

2. Read the following:

   Robert E. Probst. *Adolescent Literature: Response and Analysis* (Charles E. Merrill, 1984), pp. 3-36.

3. Make a list of the information, experiences, and feelings (such as knowledge of the landscape and how it feels to be in danger) that students should have had in order to read the story successfully. Put a check by those you think most ninth graders would have.

What Do You Think Of Doing The Following?

1. Lecturing the class on the evils of reading "trash," concentrating on magazines like those Jack and Sandra were reading.

2. Reading "To Build a Fire" aloud to the class and beginning the discussion again.

3. Showing a movie on life in the Yukon as an introduction to the story.

4. Trying the same approach with another short story such as "The Lottery" by Shirley Jackson.

5. Preparing a list of questions for students to answer as they read the story, the questions designed to help them have purposes for their reading and related to your lesson objectives.

6. Leading the class through a directed reading and thinking activity (DRTA) in which you read short section, stop, ask the students to predict what will happen next, continue reading, and repeat the cycle.

Now Write A Description Of How You Would Introduce And Teach "To Build A Fire"

Explain Why You Would Do That

One More Thing You Might Do

Read E. J. Farrell, "Listen My Children and You Shall Read," *English Journal*,
January, 1966, pp. 39-45, 68.
     Note the dramatic examples that Farrell gives of how to and how not
to introduce students to literature about characters removed from their experience.

CASE 12

Heterogeneous Grouping

Because of pressure from minority groups in the school district and an egalitarian Social Studies Department, your school has stopped grouping or tracking students according to ability measured by either grades or standardized tests.

The anti-grouping people argued that it is better socially and intellectually for students to be in heterogeneous classes. They cited a few studies done of schools where student achievement had risen after ability grouping had been dropped. The gains were especially great among students who had been previously placed in so-called slow tracks. "Students live up to our expectations for them," George Marshall, a leader of the antis had maintained just before the final vote. "And we expect poor performance from students in so-called 'low' groups. We have to break that cycle of low expectation and low performance." There had been cheers, as well as a few boos.

The defenders of ability grouping warned that bright students would be bored and slow ones lost in most classes, since teachers would probably aim their lessons at the average students. They especially warned that the regular literature curriculum would be too difficult for the slow students and that disciplinary problems would, therefore, increase. "Students have plenty of chances to mix with people from other backgrounds and abilities," Margaret Hatcher had argued. "In class, they need to compete with other students who will challenge them. It's that way in tennis and in the rest of life." Aside from a few positive mutters, her last effort to state the case for grouping had been met with silence.

The vote against grouping was decisive.

In the fall, therefore, when you meet your students, three sophomore classes and two junior classes, you find from giving them diagnostic reading and writing assignments that some students in every class are barely literate and some possess college-level skills. Although you voted against ability grouping, you now wonder how you are going to accommodate the learning needs and interests of all your students.

A Few Questions You Might Ask Yourself

1. How does ability grouping affect a student's social, psychological, intellectual, and linguistic development?

2. How does ability grouping affect an English teacher's attitudes toward students? How would it affect your repertoire of teaching strategies?

3. How often should all your students in a class be doing the same assignments?

4. What kinds of assignments are likely to be successful as large-group or whole-class activities?

5. What kinds of activities are likely to be more successful if undertaken as small-group or individualized assignments?

Some Things You Might Do Next

1. Consider what the slower students in a heterogenous class might be interested in reading and writing about. Make a list of topics. Could you organize the entire class around those topics?

2. Read chapters one and four in *Student-Centered Language Arts Curriculum K-13* (Houghton Mifflin, 1968), pp. 3-9 and 45-66. The author, James Moffett, advocates heterogeneous grouping to promote a rich and diverse linguistic experience for students.

3. Explore the use of oral activities for the slow readers: make a list of ways in which these students could learn by listening and talking. Consider how you might arrange for these students to learn in this way while other students are reading and writing.

4. Identify several adults who might have been like those slow students when they were in school. Interview one or two concerning their memories of English classes.

What Do You Think Of Doing The Following?

1. Using at least half of the periods for individualized study or group projects and the other half for large-group activities.

2. Breaking the class into reading groups based on the students' interests and reading speeds.

3.   Using more audiovisual and lecture methods to keep all the students together. Providing the class with synopses of the great books and plays under study, thus providing a necessary common cultural experience for citizenship in a democratic society.

4.   Experimenting with group interaction techniques to promote interpersonal harmony and sensitivity.

5.   Encouraging cooperative learning by having students work in pairs or groups made up of equal numbers of slow and advanced students, so that the slower students receive individual tutoring and the accelerated ones practice teaching as they learn.

What Would You Do About The Great Variety Of Student Ability In Your Classes?

Explain Why You Would Do That

One More Thing You Might Do

Read

      Patricia Kelly, Mary Pat Hall, and Robert Small. "Composition through the Team Approach," *English Journal*, September, 1984, pp. 71-74.

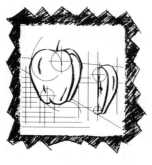

CASE 13

Forgotten Words

At the beginning of the school year, the English Department in your school voted unanimously to make increasing students' vocabularies a prime objective for the year. Enthusiastically, you voted yes. Knowing the meaning of more words was like the famed "mother and apple pie." Who could be against improved vocabularies?

You began the year with a program of new words that had been suggested by your colleagues. The program had been developed by a well-known professor and approved by the School Board. You felt confident that it would work.

Following the Vocabulary Building Program, at the beginning of each week you gave the students a list of twenty words and sent them home to look up the definitions and write sentences using each of the words. A couple of days later, you called on various students to read the definitions and the sentences that they had composed. Then you discussed each word briefly. Occasionally, as suggested by the program, you added words from the literature text, from the students' compositions, and from the newspaper. On "vocabulary day," you asked the students to give you the sentences they wrote using the words on the list. You also asked them to present words that they had encountered that weren't on the list but were new to them. A few students contributed words, but most remained silent.

At the end of each week, you gave a test in which the students had to write the definition of each word from that week's list and again use it in a sentence. To be sure that you maintained standards, you set a passing level that required each student to write, correctly, the definition for at least eighteen of the twenty words on the list and the sentences using them.

As the year has progressed, three results of this program have become obvious to you.

First, the students find the exercises tedious. They don't like looking up the words in the dictionary, and they don't understand very well the definitions they find there. You discover that grading definitions copied from dictionaries and stiff, unnatural sentences using those words is at least as boring for you as it must have been for the students writing those exercises.

Second, the grades you have to give on those exercises are usually very high. Even the poorest students seem to be able to copy definitions and write dull sentences using the words you have assigned. Indeed, your best students seem to be the only ones who, sometimes, fail the tests, because the meanings of three of the words escape them and they merely leave those blank.

But worst of all, you discover that the students almost never use the words from their vocabulary study in the class discussions or in their writing. Realizing that a word learned is only important if it is used, you have watched closely what your students say and write. *Calculation* and *demarcation* have not turned up, though you looked for them because they are on the vocabulary list for the class. No student has used *recumbant* or *statutory*, although you explained those words in class and tested on them.

You conclude that your students could use those words if they just would use them: perhaps obstancy keeps them from employing their new vocabulary. Angry and frustrated, you decide to force your students to use the words that you have taught them.

After a great deal of effort, you make an assignment that will require that the students use at least twenty of the words they have studied so far this year. The topic: "Monuments to War Heroes." The assignment: "Correctly use at least twenty of the words from the vocabulary list in the paper." You announce that the grade will be based both on the quality of the composition and the *correct* use of the vocabulary words.

On Sunday, after finishing the newspaper, you pour yourself a final cup of coffee and settle down to evaluate the compositions.

Four hours later, you throw the last paper onto the floor. Never have you read a worse set of compositions, and you've read plenty of bad ones: total confusion, misuse of many words, strained sentences, incredible awkwardness. Two of your best students rebelled against the assignment, refused to do it, and wrote about their own hero, carefully avoiding every word on the vocabulary list. Just as bad, watching for the use of those vocabulary words slowed your reading and, more frustrating, kept you from concentrating on what the students were trying to say.

Although you feel sure that your original idea to encourage the *use* of the words was correct, you conclude that the means that you used just didn't work. Was the assignment a bad one? you wonder. Or is there something wrong with the whole approach to vocabulary that you've been using? Just how can you help your students add words to their vocabularies?

A Few Questions You Might Ask Yourself

1. How do you think a person's vocabulary is formed? What causes a word to be added to it?

2. What does "knowing" a word mean? People have words they recognize but never use; words they use in writing but not in speaking and in speaking but not in writing; words they use on certain occasions but not others. What are the implications for vocabulary teaching?

3. Why didn't the students use in their writing the words they studied on the lists?

4. What kinds of new words would high school students be most likely to remember? To use?

5. What words do you know well because of your profession, hobbies, nationality, religion, or hometown that other people may not know?

Some Things For You To Do Next

1. Discuss with some friends for whom English has not been a major study how they remember learning the words they use. Ask about words they have recently added to their vocabularies. See if you can detect a pattern.

2. Make a list of ten words you do not know the meanings of (try a Victorian novel as a source). Look them up, copy the definitions, and use each in a sentence. Did you enjoy the process? Was the dictionary definition adequate to allow you to use the word with confidence? How many do you think you will remember in a week?

3. Take a survey of some students from a local high school to see how many know the meanings of the following: *foul ball, pollution, accelerator, recycle, inflation.* Consider the results.

4. Ask your colleagues how often they actually use a thesaurus and why.

What Do You Think Of Doing The Following?

1. Spending a class period before each test going over the words and their meanings.

2. Assigning your students to interview people in different occupational or recreational settings and to make a list of the words, with their working definitions, necessary for thriving in those settings.

3. Beginning to include five words from previous lists on each test to force the students to review.

4. Giving the students lessons and practice in word analysis and context clues.

5. Noting on their papers places where students could have improved their writing by the use of the right word at the right time. Then asking them to rewrite the passages using other words which are less familiar but more accurate.

6.   Instead of writing sentences with new words, having your students act out scenes in which through mime or dialogue they illustrate the meanings of selected words.

Now, Write Out A Plan To Improve Your Students' Vocabularies

Explain Why You Would Do That

One More Thing You Might Do

Keep a close look on your own vocabulary for several weeks to see how you add
words, how many and what kind you do add, and how permanent the additions
are. Case 14: Teaching the Novel

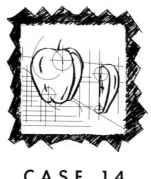

Teaching the Novel

In the English Department office, you approach your veteran colleagues with anxiety about your next unit, a study of Charles Dickens' *Great Expectations*.

"Help! Last year when I assigned *To Kill a Mockingbird*, I had the students read it in sections and discuss it chapter by chapter. Some students read ahead, finished the book, and were bored by the class discussions. Others were always behind. I'm about to teach *Great Expectations*, and I'm afraid of the worst. Anyone got any suggestions?"

You receive the following comments:

"That's the trouble with large classes. You just can't keep them together on long works. That's why I prefer teaching poems and short stories," says Jim Smith.

"I assign novels weeks ahead of time so everyone finishes the book before we start discussing it. I give a factual test just prior to our formal discussion of the book as a whole, just to check that they have indeed finished," adds Mary Wagoner.

"I pass out a complete list of characters and a plot summary to help them read. And contrary to the ideas of my college English professors, I even encourage them to use something like *Cliff's Notes*," Lynn Hall comments.

Liz Hope, one of the canniest of your colleagues, says, "I've taught novels chapter by chapter, and I've taught them as a whole. The first methods takes forever and seems to keep the class focussed on questions of plot and character. The second jumps them into higher-level questions of interpretation, theme, and evaluation of the quality of the work in comparison to other texts. I like the latter method," she says, "but younger and immature readers have trouble with it."

As you consider you own goals for teaching *Great Expectations*, you begin listing your options, hoping to make a rational plan.

A Few Questions You Might Ask Yourself

1.   How should novels be read and discussed -- in sections or as whole units? To what extent does an answer to that question depend on the novel itself (its length and difficulty), on the reading abilities of the students, or on your major objectives in teaching any given novel?

2.   How could you introduce *Great Expectations* to prepare and aid your students as they read? What kind of background do they need on the setting, language, and author?

3.   How should your approach in teaching *Great Expectations* differ from that of a history teacher directing a study of nineteenth-century England? How much time should you give to a discussion of the content of the novel as opposed to its literary elements?

4.   What kind of critical approaches should you emphasize (reader based, text based, old, new)? What emphasis should you give to eliciting different kinds of student responses described by many researchers: personal, descriptive, interpretive, evaluative?

Some Things You Might Do Next

1. Rent and view the 1967 Warner Brothers film *Up the Down Staircase* and observe how Sandy Dennis as Miss Barrett introduces Dickens' *A Tale of Two Cities*.

2. Review *Great Expectations* to discover the major questions it raises for readers in terms of interpretation of specific characters and events and in terms of the book's overall meanings.

3. Consider the difficulties which might face American teenagers in reading *Great Expectations* in terms of vocabulary, the twists of plot, and the value conflicts within and among the characters. Consider what kinds of experiences or problems in their lives can be related to the book.

What Do You Think Of Doing The Following?

1. Teaching the book in sections because Dickens' chapters were often written as self-contained serial installments and do permit individual consideration.

2. Making the students who read ahead promise not to spoil the book for those who haven't finished by telling them what happens.

3. Focusing class discussions on how and why Dickens constructed *Great Expectations* the way he did, noting his original and revised endings, rather than on rehashing the plot.

4. Discussing the book only after all have finished it, and beginning the discussion with a review of their individual written reactions to the questions "In what ways does Pip change as a person from the beginning of the novel to the end? In what ways does he remain the same?"

5. Deciding arbitrarily to teach some novels as a whole, and some section by section, in order to discover through experimentation which method you like best.

Now, Write A Plan For Teaching Great Expectations **In Sections Or As A Whole After The Students Have Finished Reading The Book**

Explain Why You Would Do That

One More Thing To Do

Read

      Susan Simmon. "Pip -- A Love Affair," *English Journal*, March, 1969, pp. 416-417

      which offers a test on *Great Expectations* that illustrates a method of helping students recognize the relationship between what they read and their own lives.

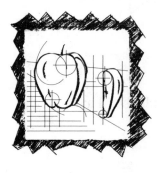

CASE 15

Monotonous Sentences

One of the most serious problems that you have detected in the writing of your upper-level eighth graders is their strong dedication to simple sentences. Although a few compound sentences pop up now and then, the complex and the compound-complex sentence seem to be unknown to these students. They have an almost fierce loyalty to the simple sentence.

Not only are the resulting papers dull reading, but the students also frequently fail to make their points clear because they have to struggle to show relationships among their ideas. More often than not, they leave the making of connections between ideas to the reader.

John Carver, a reasonably bright guy, is a good example. His last composition began

> A job on a farm is full of excitement. It also is
> hard work. Farm work means long hours and a
> lot of work. A worker must work hard to keep
> the farm going well. A farm worker must
> sometimes be a mechanic and many other things.

It continued in much the same way, its dullness and awkwardness caused by John's insistence on placing every idea in a single, separate, simple declarative sentence.

Before the assignment that produced John's simple sentences, you had tried to remedy the problem by teaching the class about the different types of sentences. Carefully, you and the class worked your way through the chapters in their grammar-composition book on different sentence patterns. For good measure, they did the exercises in the book on sentence variety, and you went over those exercises in class. Most of the students did well on the exercises in identification of types of sentences, and you had hopes that you had found the answer.

The next papers, when they came in, revealed little noticeable improvement: witness John's paper on farms. Before they write another paper, you are determined to expand their use of the various sentence patterns and types; but, other than reviewing the grammar lessons that didn't work before, you are puzzled about what to do.

A Few Questions You Might Ask Yourself

1. Why do the students choose simple sentences? Do you think they use simple sentences in speech? What are the virtues of simple sentences?

2. Do you think the ideas the students are trying to express -- use John's paper as an example -- more suitable to simple sentences or to some other type?

3. Why do you think the lesson from the grammar book didn't cause the students to change the types of sentences they use?

4. How did you learn to use the more complicated sentence types with confidence and success?

Some Things For You To Do Next

1. Read the chapters on the types of sentences and sentence variety in a standard grammar-composition series and do some of the exercises.

2. Examine a recent piece of your own writing. What sentence types do you use? How frequently? How effectively? How do you decide to employ a certain sentence type?

3. Take several of your own nonsimple sentences, break them apart into the simple sentences a student might write, and ask yourself how you put them together. How did you decide what kind of details to include? Do there seem to be any patterns involved? How might you get a student to go through the same process?

4. Read the following:

    James Moffett Ch. 5: "Grammar and the Sentence," in *Teaching the Universe of Discourse* (Houghton Mifflin, 1983), pp. 155-187.

What Do You Think Of Doing The Following?

1. Using an opaque projector to analyze for the class the sentence structure of several of the students' papers, explaining how the ideas in the sentences relate and demonstrating how the sentences might be combined.

2. Examining the structure of the sentences from magazines and newspapers brought in by the students; then asking the students to find paragraphs from

their favorite books or magazines which contain examples of the different
types of sentences and examining these examples.

3.   Marking the places in the students' next compositions where more complex
     sentences should have been used and having the students rewrite the papers
     making suitable changes.

4.   Giving the students exercises in which they have to combine a number of
     short simple sentences into one more complex sentence.

Now, What Would You Do To Improve Your Students' Sentences?

Explain Why You Would Do That

One More Thing You Might Do

Examine the following:

William Strong *Practicing Sentence Options* (Random House, 1984).

Why Can't We Read What We Want to Read?

Your assignment of the next three chapters in *The Scarlet Letter* has been ignored by at least half of the students in your better-than-average junior English class.

What did they do last night? You wonder, then decide you are better off not knowing.

The resulting class discussion is especially feeble. It quickly becomes clear that among those who hadn't read the chapters are many of your more perceptive students.

Irritated, you stop the proceedings and deliver a typical teacher sermon about duty, responsibility, the need to learn, grades, and great literature.

When you finish, there is a moment of silence; and then Jane, one of the best students in the class and one of the few who seemed to have read the assignment, raises her hand.

"I read the assignment," she says, "but I certainly didn't want to. I like to read. You know that, but I like to read what I want to read. As long as we're reading, why can't we read more of what we want to read?" Having worked herself up to this, she continues, "Why should I have to read this book when I'm not in the mood for it? You keep saying you want us to enjoy literature and learn to appreciate it. Making all of us read the same stuff at the same time whether we want to or not isn't going to do that!"

The rest of the class seems to agree, and that agreement seems to be sincere. Bob jumps in at once: "Yeah, why do we always have to read the things you pick for us? Why can we read some of things we want to read. We should be able to decide for ourselves." Todd, a quiet kid, but one of the brightest in the school, adds his voice, "If I have to read a novel, I'd rather read something by Asimov or the *Dune* series over again. They've got ideas about where our world's going."

His words make you remember your own experience reading what didn't interest you when there were other books you wanted to read but couldn't find time for. In fact, in junior high school, you'd wanted to read only science fiction just like Todd.

Although you find yourself agreeing with Jane and Todd, you see problems: students not reading or reading the same kind of book over and over, your having to read everything they read so you can check on the reading, trying to grade students on such work. You've heard of "individualized reading," but you wonder whether it really works.

A Few Questions You Might Ask Yourself

1. What are the reasons for teaching the same works of literature to all students in a class?

2. The students seem to be saying that people should be free to read the works of literature that they feel like reading. Do you agree?

3. Do you think students would read if they were free to choose the works? Would they read what English teachers would want them to read? Would they read in the way English teachers would want?

4. How could you help students find books to read? How could you help students learn to find such books for themselves?

5. Would you, as teacher, have to read or to have read all the works read by the students in an individualized program? What other problems do you see for the teacher in such a program?

6. How could you monitor and grade such reading? How do teachers grade the more conventional study of literature?

Some Things For You To Do Next

1. Read the following:

    Arthea J. S. Reed "Individualized Reading," in *Reaching Adolescents: The Young Adult Book and the School* (Holt, Rinehart and Winston, 1985), pp. 255-260.

    Lyman C. Hunt, Jr. "Six Steps to the Individualized Reading Program (IRP)," *Elementary English*, January, 1971, pp. 27-32.

2. Make a list of works of literature you have wanted to read during the last six months. Then make a list of those you have actually read. Is one list noticeably better in any way?

3. Find two friends both of whom recently have read a work of literature which you have not read and know little about. See if you can discuss the work with them in a way that produces a satisfactory discussion for all of you without your having to read the work. What kinds of questions did you ask? What problems arose?

4. Visit a school which has an individualized reading program and discuss it with the teachers and students.

What Do You Think Of Doing The Following?

1. Establishing a requirement that students read each month at least one book of their choosing but approved in advance by you, the reading to be in addition to the regular literature study.

2. Pointing out to the students that there is a difference between the study of great works and casual reading and that they are in school to learn.

3. Arranging for one class period per week to be devoted to silent reading by the students of anything they wish to read.

4. Periodically arranging for a day in which students share their responses to their individual reading.

5. Preparing a list of generic questions students can answer in writing, small groups, or a conference with you to demonstrate their understanding of individually chosen books.

6. Preparing yourself to meet students in individual conferences by reviewing references such as Donald Gollo, ed., *Books for You* (NCTE, 1986).

Now, Assume You Decide To Try An Individualized Reading Program For One Marking Period, And Describe The Kind Of Program You Would Set Up

Explain Why You Would Choose This Plan

One More Thing You Might Do

Examine the following:

> Daniel Fader et al. *The New Hooked on Books* (Berkley, 1976).

and

> Chapters V and VI in E. D. Hirsh, Jr.s *Cultural Literacy -- What Every American Needs To Know* (Houghton Mifflin, 1987).

CASE 17

Declining Reading Scores

You and your fellow English teachers have come under heavy community and administrative criticism because the mean reading scores for high school students on the state achievement test have dropped significantly for the second straight year, even though the socio-economic backgrounds of the student body have remained relatively constant. When the scores appeared in the local newspaper, Mr. Revere, the principal, called a meeting of the English and guidance departments: "Aren't you alarmed by these scores? What are you going to do about them? See what happens when we don't stress the classics?"

There is a remedial specialist in the school, generally regarded by your colleagues as competent, who works with students referred to her by teachers and counselors. There is also a course in reading improvement taught as preparation for college board tests. To the principal's challenge, various people responded by denying the validity of the tests. Your colleague John Brisk complained about being a scapegoat for a problem that teachers in all departments should be sharing. "What we need is a school-wide program in developmental reading," he proposed. One of the guidance counselors, Susan Crawford, suggested a more drastic step: bringing in a performance contracting team of experts to coordinate a new intensive effort in reading, using materials similar to those found in the SRA lists.

But these suggestions bother you. You remember reading a study that demonstrated the advantages of a program requiring extensive rapid reading of many books when compared to the usual program of fewer texts studied intensively under the teachers' direction. You agree with the results of that study: you believe that the way to learn to read is to read.

But how should your department respond to your principal?

A Few Questions You Might Ask Yourself

1. What are you doing in your classes which might improve or impede reading abilities?

2. What kinds of reading abilities do standardized tests measure? What do the individual guidance folders show about the development of a student's reading abilities through the grades?

3. What are the teachers in other subject areas doing to teach reading?

4. What do the writers and researchers in reading and English say teachers should do to stimulate reading growth?

Some Things You Might Do Next

1. Obtain a copy of a standardized test of reading given to junior high or high school students (try the teachers of a teaching of reading class or the

curriculum lab). Analyze the content of the reading passages and the questions on those passages.

2.   Examine the literature and reading textbook used in a nearby school. Compare the content and subject matter of the literature selections to the content in the reading test. Compare the questions in the literature text with those in the test.

3.   Examine the following:

      Thomas H. Estes and Joseph L. Vaughn *Reading and Learning in the Classroom* (Allyn & Bacon, 1985).

What Do You Think Of Doing The Following?

1.   Asking the board of education to authorize an all-out effort to reduce by 50% the time parents allow students to watch television.

2.   Accompanying all reading assignments with study or guide questions to be completed for homework.

3.   Giving your students weekly tests on finding the main ideas in articles from *Time* or *Newsweek* so they become test-wise.

4. Lobbying for the elimination of standardized tests on grounds of unreliability and invalidity.

5. Inviting a consultant from a speed-reading program to teach the department how to teach students to increase speed and comprehension.

6. Increase the practice of oral reading in class by your students.

Now, Describe The Plan You Would Propose To Your Principal To Raise The Students' Reading Scores

Explain Why You Would Propose That Plan

One More Thing You Might Do

Examine the following:

Richard C. Anderson et al. *Becoming a Nation of Readers* (National Academy of Education, 1984).

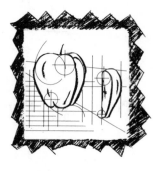

Mechanical Errors in Writing

Comfortably settled at home, you begin the marking and grading of the second set of compositions from your rather slow ninth-grade class. The first set was terrible, and you carefully indicated all of the errors in each paper. Before you handed them back, you told the class that they could rewrite the papers to improve their grades.

In class, you discussed certain errors that seemed to be present in many of the compositions. You used examples taken from the students' papers. Then you assigned the sections in the grammar-composition book that related to those errors and had the students do the exercises in those sections. Finally, the students rewrote their papers, and you reread them. They did seem improved, although you weren't sure how much of the improvement came from the students' review of the grammar book and how much resulted from the marking you had done on the earlier versions.

But now you hope to see the product of your labors. The assignment: "Write about something, not a person but something a person uses, like a hammer, or a part of a person, like a face or hand. You may pretend to be the thing and write from its point of view, or you may write about it from the outside."

The first paper you pick up is by Joey Snyder, a good-natured kid but one who seems to get into trouble most days without meaning to. As you begin to read, you remember his last paper as one of the poorest in the class.

> At first it was in a ocean and from the ocean I
> went to a lack and then in a creek and on to river.
> One nice day the son rose up and pull me up in
> the sky to a cloud first it was hot and nice and
> all of a sudden it was very cold and we was very
> cold and fall and then we hit a cold air and fall
> and then fall on the ground and we was snow.

Displeased, you put Joey's paper down without a mark and pick up the next one on the pile. It's by Jane Berry, a serious, hard-working student without much imagination. You expect it be rather dull but at least correctly written.

> There are many kinds of hands on the earth.
> Some hands show hate or love. But most of
> them show work.   Where can you see lots of
> hands? Well, someday go someplace where a lot
> of people go like a ballgame or a mall or the best
> place would be a school. They will be all kinds,
> different of course. Their are hands of women
> who do hard work cooking of course their's will
> be like rough and red and cracked unless they use
> creams. So you can see the many different kinds
> of hands in the worl.

Quickly you skim the rest. The sad truth is that there is no noticeable improvement in the papers. If anything, there seem to be more errors in mechanics and spelling, almost as if the attention you paid to correctness had made the writing worse. And the papers are shorter than the last set and seem, somehow, to show less of the students' personalities. You hate to admit it, but Joey's paper, for all its errors, is probably the most interesting of the set.

It cost you the better part of a Saturday to mark the previous set of papers and several class periods to discuss the errors, and no improvement has resulted. You can tell that if you mark these papers in the same way, you'll have to give them several hours. And, if you go over them in class, you'll end up talking about the same comma mistakes and run-on sentences, assigning the same parts of the grammar book. You wonder if, after doing all that again, the same lack of improvement will result. It makes you tired to think of it. And what can you do instead that might have some chance of working?

A Few Questions You Might Ask Yourself

1. How bad are the papers? How would you describe their chief faults? Are there any good aspects to them? How would you describe the good points?

2. How well should you expect ninth-grade students to write? What kind of writing problems would you expect them to have?

3. What system of marking or commenting on errors should you use?

4. What would you hope would happen when you indicate the weaknesses and errors on papers? Why do you think it didn't it happen with this set of papers?

5. What kinds of writing assignments are most likely to produce good writing? Consider how the error rate of papers might vary when students write personal versus impersonal papers. What do you think will be the effect of varying the purpose, the situation, and the audience on the number of mechanical errors?

Some Things For You To Do Next

1. Using a red pen, mark every error, awkwardness, organizational problem, etc. in Joey's paper. Then try to look at it as if it were your paper.

2. Using some color other than red, comment on the good points -- well-chosen words, good phrases, examples of sentence variety, etc. -- in Jane's paper. Make the comments genuine but enthusiastic, and remember that the paper was written by a ninth-grader. Then consider how you would feel if it were your paper and you received it back from a teacher marked in this way. Now, using the red pen, mark all the errors in Jane's paper. Would you react differently to receiving this paper back if you were the author?

3. Using a third color, mark the places in each paper where an error (as opposed to something not being fully developed) actually causes you to have difficulty understanding what the student was trying to say. How many are there?

4. Read Mina Shaunessy's suggestions for coding errors into manageable types in *Errors and Expectations* (Oxford University Press, 1977), pp. 14-43.

5. Teachers have for generations taught both traditional Latinate and modern transformational grammar with the hope that such instructions would reduce their students' syntactical and mechanical errors. Read Frank O'Hare's review of reseach on this practice in his *Sentence Combining: Improving Student Writing Without Formal Grammar Instruction* (Research Report No. 15) (Urbana, Ill.: NCTE 1973, pp. 5-18.

What Do You Think Of Doing The Following?

1. Turning the papers back to the students unmarked, telling them how terrible their work is, and having the papers rewritten.

2. Marking the errors again carefully and arranging for individual conferences with the students one by one to discuss their work.

3. Dividing the students into groups to examine and discuss each other's papers
    and making yourself available for any student who would like advice.

4. Dividing the students into pairs to proofread each other's papers, each student
    to receive a mechanics grade for the paper he or she proofread.

Now, Write How You Would Handle Students' Papers

Explain Why You Would Do That

One More Thing You Might Do

Read the following:

> Ken Macrorie "To Be Read" in Richard L. Graves, ed., *Rhetoric and Composition* (Hayden Book Company, 1984), pp. 81-88.

CASE 19

Exasperating Exams

You are enthusiastic while planning and teaching your literature classes and units, and your students are usually eager and attentive, especially the first semester. Both you and your students, however, get exasperated when test times come. They never seem to do as well on your tests as you think they should, judging from their performance during class, and many also don't do as well on their tests as they do on standardized tests. Their poor performance bothers you, and it causes them to lose interest and at times to become hostile. Often you're tempted to give all A's and B's just to maintain student enthusiasm, but you believe students should earn their grades so that the workers are rewarded and the loafers revealed. You can't understand why you have to scale your grades, why your hard workers often do worse than many of your slackers.

Looking for a solution to the problem, you study your objectives for the next unit.

Objectives:

1. Students will be able to state in their own words what happens to the major characters in *Great Expectations*.

2. Students will be able to explain how the actions of the major characters affect the actions and feelings of other characters.

3. Students will be able to describe how the characters develop and to argue whether they are developed as sympathetic or unsympathetic characters.

4. Students will be able to state what they think are the major themes of *Great Expectations* and to argue whether or not they think Dickens succeeded aesthetically in dramatizing his resolutions of these themes.

You feel you need to plan more carefully how you're going to evaluate the students on this unit so you can be sure the students have every chance to learn the things they're going to be tested on. You have to decide what kinds of tests, items, or questions you can develop to assess your students' achievement of these objectives. And you need to decide how you will weight these objectives in the final grades.

A Few Questions You Might Ask Yourself

1. What are your purposes in testing? What are your purposes in asking any given question?

2. Which is more reliable, students' daily performance or their test performance? What are some possible reasons for discrepancies in these kinds of performances?

3. What do you think your questions should be measuring: recall, interpretation, explication of new material, or application of literary concepts?

4. How should examination questions in a literature class differ from those asked in a history or science class?

5. How much relative weight should you assign to grades on quizzes versus unit tests?

Something You Might Do Next

1. Read the following:

    Alan Purvis "Evaluation of Learning in Literature" in Benjamin Bloom et al., *Handbook on Formative and Summative Evaluation of Student Learning* (McGraw-Hill, 1971), pp. 697-766.

2. Do an item analysis of a corrected test you took recently to find which kind of items were the most troublesome for you. Are the questions precisely worded to avoid confusing the students?

3. Examine several tests in the teachers' manuals of literature anthologies. How many questions ask for factual information? How many require analysis? Making a judgment? Stating a response?

What Do You Think Of Doing The Following?

1. Reviewing each test question with the class and having students hand in their corrected responses to raise their grades.

2. Adopting the kinds of tests used by many college English professors: 50% identification and explication of selected passages and 50% essay.

3.   Making all tests on literature open-book and take-home.

4.   Abolishing all objective tests on literature.

5.   Replacing tests with other assignments: papers, oral reports, short quizzes, reading journals or logs.

Now, Write Out Specific Items -- Both Short Answers And Essay -- For The Objectives Listed For Great Expectations **Or Another Novel You Are Teaching**

Explain Why You Developed The Items You Did And How You Would Weight Them For Credit

One More Thing To Do

Take the test yourself. In particular, note how long it takes you to write satisfactory answers to your own essay questions.

Elitism in the School Literary Magazine

Billy Barrons, a representative of the school's literary magazine, comes to your class to take orders for this year's edition. He is met by mumbles and grumbles.

Sam Kelly challenges, "Why should we buy *Highlights*? Only people from the higher classes get to write for it."

Billy rebuts, "That's not so. Anyone can submit poetry or fiction."

Sherry Snyder joins the argument. "Yeah, but if you're not on the editorial board or one of the in-crowd, good luck to you."

Billy explains, "Miss Elliot, our advisor, supervises the selections."

Sam snorts, "Ha! I got in her class by mistake last year. She only likes way-out modern poetry about weird feelings and ideas. I never buy it."

At this point, you step in to start the class and end the argument. As the representative leaves, he chides the class for lack of school spirit and reminds everyone how many awards *Highlights* has won for its cover and layout.

Your students ask you whether they should write for the magazine or even subscribe to it. You sidestep these questions and spend part of your evening studying old editions of *Highlights*. Some of the selections are strikingly original, many more are pedestrian or as obscure as your students had charged. You feel certain that many of your students, even those not in your advanced classes, have written, and can write, well enough to be published. Should you try to help your students get into *Highlights*?

A Few Questions You Might Ask Yourself

1. What should be the purposes and benefits of a school literary magazine?

2. What should be the relationship between writing in the literary magazine and the writing done for classes?

3. What should be the procedures and criteria for selecting works to be published?

4. Would it be feasible to publish dittoed copies of student writing from each class so that every student gets to see something he or she has written?

Some Things For You To Do Next

1. Examine a school literary magazine. What kinds of selections are included? How well written are they? What assignments might have been given in a class that would produce such writing?

2. Interview the sponsor of a school literary magazine to discover how the published works are selected.

3. Consider what would be involved in setting up a class literary magazine to publish your students' work that doesn't make the school magazine.

4. Prepare three writing assignments that you think will call for imaginative rather than expository writing.

What Do You Think Of Doing The Following?

1. Using at least one day every two weeks for creative writing and submitting all of the papers to the literary magazine.

2. Starting another or "underground" magazine as an outlet for your proletarian writers.

3. Asking the local Rotarians to sponsor a short story writing contest.

4. Regularly dittoing and distributing the writing of all your students.

5. Following reading assignments with the option of writing a creative paper in
    the same genre as the selection instead of requiring the usual critical
    expositions on the assigned text.

Now, Describe How You Will Respond To Your Students' Questions About Their Work Appearing In The Literary Magazine.

Explain Why You Would Do That

One More Thing You Might Do

Examine several of the journals listed below that publish student writing:

Literary Cavalcade (Scholastic Magazines, Inc.)

Criquet (Open Court Publishing Company)

Young Authors' Magazine (Theroplan, Inc.)

Pennywhistle Press (Gannet Co., Inc.)

Young American (Young American Publishing Co.)

Bittersweet (Lebanon High School, Lebanon, Mo.)

Foxfire (B. Eliot Wigginton, Roban Gap, Ga.)

Seventeen (Seventeen Magazine)

Hanging Loose (Robert Hershon et al., Brooklyn, N.Y.)

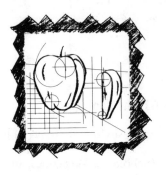

The Few
Who Answer

"Why do you think Bobby decides 'to tough this out' himself?" you ask your slow tenth-grade class. They have been reading Fran Arrick's *Chernowitz* and have gotten to the place where Bobby decides to deal in that way with the boys who are picking on him.

Three hands go up: Jane, Susan, and Henry.

You wait.

"Come on now," you encourage; "the author gives us plenty to go on."

Slowly, Mary and George raise their hands. Jane, Susan, Henry, Mary, and George -- the same hands you always see whenever you ask a question, the same five students who always answer and always answer correctly.

For some weeks at the beginning of school, you felt pleased with yourself for prompting such good discussions in your third-period class. Slow tenth graders are, according to many teachers, impossible to get to participate. But in this class, there always seemed to be a response and a free interchange among the students.

Then, one day in mid-October, you began to suspect that only the same five students actually said much in class, with a few others adding a comment on occasion. You began watching more carefully who spoke and who didn't. Then came the day that Jane, Susan, and George were all absent, and the true situation became vividly clear as the class limped painfully through a discussion of "The Road Not Taken" -- or, really, a nondiscussion.

At any rate, you see plainly that, while the faithful five discuss and argue freely, the other members of the class sit back quietly and listen, or, at least, pretend to listen.

You have tried calling on other students; but, although they can answer more or less successfully about half the time, the result of your calling on students has been painful, more an oral quiz than the true exchange of responses and ideas that you want. You ask questions; they give the briefest answers they think you'll let them get away with. By not calling on the faithful five, you've eliminated any interchange, and even the faithful five have begun to sit back and wait for you to decide who will be permitted to answer.

There must be some way to draw more of the students into discussions, but you have to admit to yourself that you haven't found the trick.

A Few Questions You Might Ask Yourself

1. What kinds of questions do teachers usually ask in English classes? What kinds of answers do they expect? What kinds of answers do students think teachers want?

2. What reasons might the silent students have for remaining silent? Could any action by the teacher meet all or most of those reasons?

3. When do most people become eager to express their thoughts and ideas? When do they keep silent even though they have something to say?

4. How does class size affect the quality and quantity of class participation?

Some Things For You To Do Next

1. Pick a fairly simple short story that you know well and like. Make a list of questions that a teacher in high school might ask about it. Examine the questions, asking yourself

    a. How would a student feel if he or she were asked each one?
    b. What would be the purpose of asking each?
    c. What kinds of students would be able to and perhaps want to answer each?
    d. Are there any kinds of students for whom none of the questions would be appropriate?

2. Watch what goes on in the next class you take. Using a simple shorthand, record who talks, to whom, and how much. Analyze the results to see if you can detect a relation between the amount of participation and any other factor such as teaching method.

3. Examine your own reaction in classes when the teachers have asked questions that any student may answer and when they have called on you for an answer.

4. Read the following:

    John H. Bushman and Kay Parks Busman. *Teaching English Creatively* (Charles C. Thomas, 1986), pp. 9-24.

What Do You Think Of Doing The Following?

1. Dividing the class into several groups for the next discussion, putting the faithful five together in one group so that the other students will have to participate.

2. Telling the class that you are going to grade on class participation and following through by letting the students know what grade they receive each week.

3. Giving the students the questions in advance so that the slower students can prepare answers and thus be more confident.

4. Making a transcript of one of your class discussions; then making a list of the questions you asked and noting which ones asked for recalling, reporting, or describing and which ones called for reflecting, applying, or evaluating.

5. Consciously making an effort to wait longer after asking a question to give students more time to respond before you push on, since studies show the longer teachers give students to formulate responses, the better the quality and quantity of thought in the responses.

Now, Describe How You Would Stimulate More Class Participation

Explain Why You Would Do That

One More Thing You Might Do

Examine the following:

Leila Christenberry and Patricia P. Kelly. *Questioning: A Path to Critical Thinking* (NCTE, 1983).

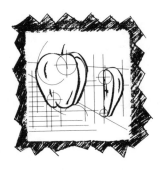

Etymology
or What's in a Name?

At the start of the school year, you ask your students to introduce themselves. As they do, you write their names on the blackboard. You then ask the class if they know why they have their names and if they know what their names mean. A few students reply. Mary Baker says she was named after her grandmother and that many generations ago, her ancestors were bakers. Cass Yardley says his grandfather legally changed his name from Jadisiewicz to Yardley because Americans couldn't spell or pronounce his original name. You then ask your class to do a little research with the help of their parents and dictionaries to find out more about their names.

You explain that this assignment is an example of etymology, the study of the origin of words, which the class will investigate for the next two weeks. "Many students have difficulty with vocabulary, so I think we'll try to analyze words more carefully to see if knowledge of etymology will help you. By the way, Hector, did you know you are living up to your name with your love of argument? Here, you can see for yourself in my copy of Wilfred Funk's *Word Origins*."

You also tell the class that they should be thinking of how new words come into the language and old words change their meanings. The class goes well and the students seem interested, but you really aren't sure where to go from here. Your textbooks have a few lessons on etymology among many more on dictionary skills. You believe etymology is interesting for its own sake, but you also believe it is important for your students to be able to choose their own words carefully, and to be aware of how politicians and advertisers choose theirs.

You've decided to begin tomorrow's class by saying, "In the beginning was *the word*, so how did lies get to be called 'disinformation'? And how did 'bad' get to be 'cool'?" So where do you go from there?

A Few Questions You Might Ask Yourself

1. How much of the history of the development of modern English would it be necessary to include in your unit?

2. How important is it for students to learn Greek and Latin roots and to know how new words come into existence ?

3. What specific words or kinds of words would you want them to study?

4. What is the relationship between etymology and semantic analysis? How do modern connotations differ from denotations of words?

Some Things To Do Next

1.   Review for yourself the principles of word making. How much do you know about this subject?

2.   Examine two examples of high school grammar-composition texts and a school dictionary to see how they treat word origins.

3.   Read

      Charlton Laird "Down Gaintwife: The Uses of Etymology," *English Journal*, November, 1970, pp. 1106-1112.

      R.C. Simonini, Jr. "Word Making in Present Day English," *English Journal*, September, 1966, pp. 752-757.

4.   Make a list of words that might relate to student interests (recreational and vocational) or that you think would be helpful to them. Look in a library for resources that would help them trace the origins of these words and their definitions.

What Do You Think Of Doing The Following?

1.   Having the students check advertising to study how and why companies give products the names they do, i.e., Ajax cleanser, Mercury Cougar, Mr. Clean, Smucker's Jelly.

2.   Having the students review the names of literary characters to see how often an author attempts to have a character's personality reflected in his or her name.

3.   Having each student select a topic of interest, i.e., cars, vocations, hobbies, or countries, and tracing the history of words related to that topic in the form of a etymological notebook. Then basing his/her grade on a test of his/her understanding of those words.

4.   Not using the etymological approach with at least one of your other classes. Instead, using a straight definitional and contextual approach to vocabulary with that class and comparing the gain in vocabulary between the two sets of classes.

5.   Having the students memorize Greek and Latin prefixes, suffixes, and roots and using this information to analyze a list of vocabulary words.

Now, Write The Outline Of A Resource Unit On Etymology That You Could Use To Supplement The Literature And Vocabulary Your Classes Will Be Studying

Explain Why You Included What You Did

One More Thing To Do

Carry out the research necessary to write the etymology of your own names (first, middle, last) or of one your own favorite words. Make a list of the steps involved and consider at what grade level students might be able to carry out a similar project.

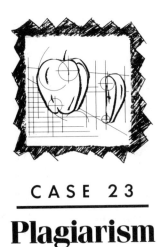

Plagiarism

Reading through a set of student papers for your seniors' outside reading project, you come to Simone Meridith's paper on the novels of Charlotte Brontë. The purpose of the paper was to interpret and evaluate the writing of a single author, and Simone has chosen Brontë. Simone's paper is, in parts, disturbingly professional. You feel certain most of the paper was not written by Simone but by a Brontë critic. Simone does use some quotations and footnotes, but only for passages from the novels.

When you read the other papers you find a few passages which seem suspiciously professional. No other student, however, has borrowed as freely as it appears Simone has. You remember students being dismissed from college for plagiarism, and you also recall the widespread practice of buying term papers from fraternity or sorority files. You are well aware that some schools and teachers take severe views of cheating and plagiarism, whereas others regard them as forgiveable or redeemable offenses.

Your school has a diffuse approach to teaching the research paper. Every department has the responsibility for teaching the conventions of writing in its own discipline. Your department, the English department, requires one major research paper each year in the academic classes, but "research" is ill-defined. Some teachers see the research paper as an opportunity for students to learn to summarize and synthesize primary and secondary sources. Others forbid the use of secondary sources and want their students to apply their own critical intelligence to the work of a single author.

Simone has usually done very good if not imaginative work. Her mother, who casually told you on parents' night that she had "honored in English at Radcliffe," seemed especially concerned that Simone excel.

What, you wonder, can I do about Simone? Should I do anything?

A Few Questions You Might Ask Yourself

1.   How well do you think most high school students understand how they should credit other writers when using their ideas and words?

2.   Why might a student deliberately plagiarize?

3.   What should a school's policy be regarding plagiarism? Should the punishment be any harsher when the student plagiarizes unintentionally? Suppose Simone says she forgot to insert the footnotes and quote those parts of her paper in question?

4.   What should the purpose of the assignment be: to (a) teach students how to express their own critical reactions to literature, (b) teach them to synthesize the ideas of professional critics, or (3) give them practice in quoting and footnoting?

5.   What should you do if you find the exact source Simone plagiarized? What if you cannot find it, but you are still sure she did not write the paper herself?

Some Things You Might Do Next

1. Read

    Doris R. Dant "Plagiarism in High School: A Survey," *English Journal,*
        February, 1986, pp. 81-84.

2. Interview one high school English teacher and one college English professor
    to see how they would handle the situation with Simone.

3. Examine *The Legal Aspects of Plagiarism* by Ralph D. Mawdsley (National
    Organization on Legal Problems in Education, 1985).

What Would You Think Of Doing The Following?

1. Setting aside a day to explain to the class what is and what is not permissable
    in using outside or secondary sources in critical papers. Explaining also the
    possible academic and legal penalties.

2. Turning the matter over for investigation to the student judiciary committee
    as mandated by the school's honor system.

3. Teaching a unit on famous literary borrowers (some would say pirates) such
    as Shakespeare and Clifford Irving. You would include such topics as
    collaboration, ghost writing, and copyright laws.

4. Making the class sign pledges not to read professional criticism until after they read a work and formulate their own reactions.

5. Asking Simone to revise her paper, include more of her own ideas, and add the footnotes she neglected in her first draft.

Write What Would You Do In Simone's Case?

Explain Why You Would Do That

One More Thing You Might Do

Examine

Frederick C. Crews, *Pooh Perplex: A Freshman Casebook* (Dutton, 1965), a satirical casebook of criticism on *Winnie-the-Pooh*.

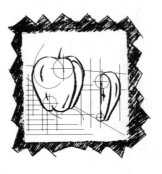

CASE 24

The Media
Are the Question

Dagmar Shore, fifteen-year-old sophomore, pleads with you not to assign reading or writing homework Thursday nights: "That's when the best TV programs are on." She is only partly kidding. You know from questionnaires that most students spend much more time watching television, listening to radios and records, reading magazines, and going to movies than they do reading books. Reminded by Dagmar of these interests, you decide to undertake a class unit on the study of the media.

You begin by asking the class to make a list of possible topics, questions, and projects as a basis for organizing the unit. For topics, the class suggests rating television dramatic series, sport specials, newscasts, and talk shows. For questions, the class lists (a) Why do people prefer television to books? (b) Is it correct that print is becoming obsolete as a form of communication? (c) Why can't teenagers see X-rated films? For projects, they suggest visiting the local television and radio stations, videotaping student productions, and making a movie about the school cafeteria.

Those seem like good ideas, but you wonder what other projects and activities involving commercial media might be worth doing for your class. You know that several of your students want to pursue acting or announcing careers and even work part-time at local stations.

When you announce that naturally you will expect them to write regular reports on their viewing and also read articles and books by media experts, the class groans, "Here we go again." Given your class's reaction to your announcement that you may turn this unit into a traditional academic exercise, should you consider other kinds of reports and presentations?

A Few Questions Which You Might Ask Yourself

1. How does the study of media relate to the traditional objectives of teaching English?

2. How could you use the resources of the school's audiovisual personnel and materials and community resources in this unit?

3. What could you do if not all students have access to televisions which receive the assigned programs? Do you think the school A.V. department would have equipment to videotape TV programs for classroom viewing?

4. Since you plan to study newspapers and magazines, which ones do you think you should order?

5. Do you have the knowledge and experience to help students make films or videotapes? If not, where could you turn for help?

Some Things You Might Do Next

1. Examine several recent issues of *Media and Methods* to see what the authors of the articles suggest should be taught to students about visual media.

2. Contact a local video store to investigate the costs of materials needed to make tapes and records and find out what resources are already available.

3. Interview a local television announcer to find out how he/she "made it" into the field.

What Do You Think Of Doing The Following?

1. Restricting the unit to one kind of media to make it more manageable.

2. Organizing the unit around the following kinds of problems: (a) To what extent are television and movies aesthetic wastelands? (b) How does advertising reflect or erode America's values? (c) Why are there so many conflicts between the media and governments?

3. Letting students do independent or group media projects of their choice after you approve a prospectus. How the press can make and unmake a president and how a TV network decides whether or not to renew a controversial show such as *Max Headroom* might be two topics you suggest.

4. Developing a list of terms or concepts related to media that students should be able to define on an objective test.

5. Requiring students to demonstrate critical and analytical viewing and reading skills by comparing and contrasting two TV shows in the same genre or two newspapers such as the *New York Times* and *USA Today*, or two cartoons such as Doonesbury and Bloom County.

Write A Set Of Objectives For The Media Unit And Develop Activities And Assignments

Defend Your Objectives And Activities

One More Thing To Do

Interview a member of a college communications department to learn what is taught in that department to prospective performers and technicians. Consider how you might adapt that program to use in high school.

Dealing with Gifted Students

When you received your class assignments last spring and saw that, at last, you had been given a "superior" class, you felt a definite sense of pleasure. Over the summer, you gathered a number of challenging activities to use with them, "to raise the curriculum to their level," as you put it to some friends.

By October, you conclude two things about that superior third-period class. First, in this school, "superior" classes -- if this class is typical -- aren't really made up of bright, talented students. Oh, the kids in the class are, on the average, a bit smarter than those in the average classes you'd been teaching and certainly brighter than the "remedial" students you'd spent so much time with over the years. But, really talented, really perceptive about writing and literature? No. The big difference between this class and the others you have taught seems to be that these kids are well behaved and do their homework. They also expect good grades for being well behaved and doing their work on time, but that is a different problem.

The other thing you conclude -- and after only a few days -- is that your "superior" class does have a few superior students, three to be exact. Pat, Allen, and Hilda are clearly much more advanced than the other students. Even though you are sure you are right about them, you ask Sue Pittman in the Guidance Office to help you check their records. Nearly perfect grade reports, high standardized test scores, and glowing comments from teachers all the way back to the first grade confirm your belief. And their English teachers from last year also praise them. As Jane Carr says of Allen and Hilda, "I just wish I had more students like them. Then a so-called superior class would be what it is supposed to be. And I also wish we had a program for the gifted and talented the way some schools have." "Gifted and talented" is clearly the term for people like Allen, Pat, and Hilda.

Knowing that you needed to do something different for them than for the other students, you decide to try using independent study with them. Bob Richards, the school assistant librarian, agrees to let them come to the library during third period to work on their special projects, and the three students seem enthusiastic. Pat and Hilda have a study hall during your planning period, so they can meet with you each week to discuss their projects. Allen can stay after school on Thursdays for a conference.

With the details worked out, you sit down with each student to decide on a project. Each of them has already settled on a topic: Hilda, a very religious girl, wants to work on sermons, comparing those of Jonathan Edwards to those of two of the more important modern preachers of her denomination. Allen plans to read the journals of William Byrd and Samuel Pepys and to keep a similar journal of his own, then write a discussion of the art of journal writing. Pat has decided to compare the short stories of Washington Irving to those of Poe.

The weekly meetings go well; and, when the first grading period is over, you collect the projects and are very pleased with the results. This seems to be the way to deal with those gifted and talented students you now have begun to hear so much about.

Before your can decide what to do next with Pat, Allen, and Hilda, several other members of the class ask where they've been all month. As you start to explain, George, a friend of Allen's, describes what Allen has been doing. "Why can't we do something like that?" a number of students ask. Your turn the discussion aside with "We'll see." But you wonder. Even the slowest students in the class have worked hard and done at least satisfactorily, although none of them has shown the flair that Hilda, Allen, and Pat have. So why shouldn't they do independent work? Could they handle it as well as the gifted and talented trio? You don't want frustration and failure to undo what you believe you've accomplished with the more or less average students in the class.

When you sit down with your three "gifted and talented students," however, and propose that they pick another project for independent study during the next grading period, both Hilda and Allen ask to come back into the class. When pressed, they admit that they miss talking with the other students. Allen, always frank, says, "Well, you see, sitting there in the library got kinda boring at times. Besides, I usually know the answers in class, and it's fun sometimes to be one of the best students, you know." Even Pat says she wouldn't mind going back into the class.

So now you have to decide. Who should do independent study? Only the gifted or all who want to? And what can you do with Hilda, Pat, and Allen to provide the extra challenge that they need?

A Few Questions You Might Ask Yourself

1. What do you think is the difference between "good" students and those that can be described as "gifted and talented"?

2. Is there any reason why independent study is more suited to the gifted and talented than to other types of students? What might they learn by doing an independent project that they would not learn in a formal class setting? What might they miss?

3.   Which is more important for successful independent study, high intelligence or conscientiousness? What kinds of students would probably do poorly under independent study?

4.   Other than independent projects in place of regular class work, how might you meet the needs of those few gifted and talented students that you have in a class made up mostly of good but not unusually talented students?

Some Things For You To Do Next

1.   Examine the following:

William W. West *Teaching the Gifted and Talented in the English Classroom* (National Education Association, 1980).

2.   Make a list of several projects you have thought about doing in the field of English but have not had time to do, for example, reading all of F. Scott Fitzgerald's novels and short stories. Consider whether or not you would actually do them thoroughly and well if you were suddenly offered both the time and freedom to do them on your own for college credit. Would doing these projects on your own benefit you more than taking college classes?

3.   Interview a friend, colleague, or acquaintance that you would describe as gifted and talented in some field such as poetry, literature, art, or acting. Ask the person to reflect on his/her secondary school experience: Did the school encourage the development of talents? Was there time in the curriculum for such development? Were special talents valued by the teachers and other students? Were independent study projects permitted? Encouraged? Was there conflict between school requirements and development of special talents? Try to find out whether the person being interviewed feels now that school contributed to the development of his/her special talents, had no effect on such development, or was an obstacle.

What Do You Think Of Doing The Following?

1.   Explaining to Allen, Hilda, and Pat that they are gifted and talented and so must use and develop their talents to the fullest and that such development can't take place in the regular class.

2. Letting everyone in the class who wants to do an independent study sign up for a library pass and encouraging Allen, Pat and Hilda also to do so.

3. Having Allen, Hilda, and Pat come back to the class and present their projects so that the other members of the class can benefit from their work.

4. Explaining to the rest of the class that Hilda, Allen, and Pat are especially gifted students, that only such students can carry out independent projects successfully, and that no one else in the class has yet shown such special talents. Then challenging them to show what they can do during the next grading period.

5. Dropping the idea of independent projects entirely but trying to be sure that you give Hilda, Allen, and Pat the most challenging questions in class discussions and the most difficult homework assignments.

6. Arrange with the guidance department to move Hilda, Allen, and Pat to another English class that is at the next higher grade level.

Now, Describe How You Would Handle The Gifted Students And The Others Who Have Asked To Do Independent Study

Explain Why You Would Handle It That Way

One More Thing You Might Do

Examine the state Department of Education requirements and guidelines for gifted and talented programs in your state if such exist. If not, examine instead a school or school system's description of its gifted and talented program. Look especially at how the gifted and talented students are described and the procedures for identifying them.

CASE 26

Complaints About Grades on Compositions

Late in the first marking period of the first semester, you begin getting complaints from some students about the grades you have been awarding their compositions: "What am I doing wrong? Miss Jones gave me A's and B's for the same kind of writing. Why are new teachers always such harsh markers?"

You know there are other English teachers who share your grading standards and practices, which you believe are fair. The particular students who complain seem to write papers which are mechanically acceptable but uninteresting, full of clichés, and void of insights.

You are willing to discuss the problem with the students and to check with their former teachers about their criteria for grading writing. You are uncomfortable, however, with the prospect of compromising your standards, especially since you suspect at least some of the complainers are just testing your toughness.

After checking with other teachers in the department, you find a diversity of criteria and grading practices. Since you are required to assign at least one written exercise a week, you are concerned as you imagine the possibility of weekly arguments over grades on papers. One of your senior colleagues, Keith Covert, tells you that he never puts a grade on a student's composition, only comments and corrections. He does, however, record grades for each paper in his gradebook. He requires students to rewrite failing papers.

Still another colleague, Jane Caldwell, grades with checks or credit/no credit for each writing assignment until the students have a portfolio of work thick enough to provide them a range of choices for ten papers they will revise later for grades. She reads the revised papers only to grade them, not to comment on them again.

To the warnings of the department chair to make sure your gradebook can document every term grade, Jane says, "No sweat. I still have plenty of grades from vocabulary, spelling, and grammar tests, even though I count them only half as much as composition grades."

"Help!" you say. "What should I do about grading?"

A Few Questions You Might Ask Yourself

1. What criteria should you use in grading compositions? To what extent should you explain them in advance to students? Should the same criteria apply equally to every paper?

2. What should be the relationship between grading and teaching writing? Between grades and comments on papers?

3. What effects do you want grades to have on your students?

4. How much time do you think most teachers spend reading, marking, and grading writing? How much time do they spend preparing writing assignments and getting the classes ready to write?

Some Things For You To Do Next

1. Examine a set of compositions from a class in a local school. Separate the papers into piles containing those which are fairly correct but dull, those which are not very correct mechanically but interesting, those that are pretty good in both ways, and those that are poor in both ways. How many are in each pile? Can you apply the same standard to all of the papers?

2. Compare your ratings of these papers to the ratings of a colleague.

3. Conduct a detailed survey of grading practices in an English department. Find out how many teachers take points off for mechanical errors as a major strategy. How many give two grades for each paper, one for content and one for form?

4. Try to put down on paper what you think each of the traditional grades (A, B, C, D, F) mean in relation to student composition.

5. Read "Grading and Evaluating" in Dan Kirby and Tom Liner, *Inside Out* (Boynton/Cook, 1981), pp. 183-202. Apply their examples of holistic scoring of essays (essay scales, analytic scales, and primary trait scales) to samples of the students' compositions you found for number 1 above.

What Do You Think of Doing The Following?

1. Continuing to use specific comments, but not putting grades on papers. Instead, write them down in your gradebook.

2. Explaining to the students that grading essays is a very subjective process and that it is up to them to meet the different standards set by different teachers.

3. Adopting the portfolio procedure suggested by James Moffett in *Student-Centered Language Arts Curriculum, K-12* (that is, not grading or even reading every single student paper, having the students read and correct each other's papers in small groups, and then selecting just a few each marking period for final revision by the student and grading by the teacher).

4. Making at least half of the writing assignments free topics to allow the creative writers a chance to be rewarded for their talents.

Prepare A Handout Describing Your Grading Criteria For Writing That You Could Distribute To Students And Parents At The Beginning Of The Year

Explain How You Would Defend Your Criteria

One More Thing To Do

Examine:
> Denny Wolfe. *Making the Grade: Evaluating and Judging Student Writing* (Coronado, 1986).

Then consider the questions: How necessary are grades? Could you use pass/fail marking? Should students be graded in terms of how they compare to other students, how much they improve, or how close they come to the performance criteria set by the assignment?

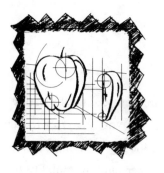

Research Papers

As a part of the curriculum for both junior and senior English, the students are supposed to write research papers either related to the literature they are studying or on a topic of personal interest. Dutifully, you assigned the papers in February to be due on the first of May and went over the chapters in the grammar-composition book on footnoting and the use of library references and sources. After several weeks, you had the students turn in brief purpose statements on the topics their papers were to deal with. Topics such as "Drugs," "Sports," "Sports Cars," and "Shakespeare" worried you, but you discussed the purposes the students had for the papers with them and hoped you had cleared up the worst problems. "After all," you told yourself, "part of doing a research paper is defining the purpose. When they get into the research, they'll work out the problems."

Now, you have finished reading the papers. With a few exceptions, the results have been disastrous. As you analyze why the papers are so bad, you see certain common problems: difficulty in finding material, topics which are too broad to deal with in a research paper, and an inability to assimilate the material read. Although you heard the students complain that neither the school library nor the town library had any material on their topics, you blamed their problems on their laziness. Now, you aren't so sure.

Worse, you realize that your lessons on narrowing a topic had little effect. A good half of the papers are on topics like Sandra's "Horses" and Mike's "Emily Dickinson's Poems" and are, consequently, impossibly general. Worst of all, about a third of the papers are merely collections of passages copied or slightly paraphrased from the magazines and encyclopedias they used in their so-called research.

Two questions face you. First, what do you do with the papers, especially the ones that are mostly based on encyclopedias? Second, what, if anything, should you do about reteaching the skills needed to write a research paper? You know you'll have to think about planning a better way for next year, but in the back of your mind is the nagging thought that writing a research paper may not be a suitable assignment for most high school students.

A Few Questions You Might Ask Yourself

1. What is a research paper? What skills does it involve? What are the reasons why students in high school might need to have those skills? Could they be learned without the writing of an actual research paper?

2. Why do you think the students had the kinds of problems they did? How could they have been avoided?

3. Can your students use interviews and field trips to gather information?

4. What kinds of inquiry skills do your students need? Are there any similarities between the scientific method and the methods a good social science or humanities researcher uses?

Some Things For You To Do Next

1. Examine some of your old research papers and consider their quality and the value to you of having done them.

2. Make a list, perhaps with the help of some friends who are neither teachers nor students, of the uses adults make of the skills learned in writing research papers. Consider how extensive these uses are.

3. Review the sections relating to research and the research paper in a high school grammar-composition book. Consider how well handled the material is. Could you write a research paper guided only by that material?

4. Check with one or more college English departments to see (a) what research skills students need to have before taking freshman English and (b) what skills are taught in that course.

5. Examine the material in one or more high school libraries and public libraries to see if the books and journals which students might need to do research for English are present.

6. Review

    Brooke Workman. *Writing Seminars in the Content Area: In Search of Hemingway, Salinger and Steinbeck* (NCTE, 1983).

What Do You Think Of Doing The Following?

1. Failing the students whose papers are mostly copied or paraphrased from encyclopedias and those whose papers are very poor, and spending the rest of the year reteaching the research paper.

2. Deciding that the problem lay in the assignment and, therefore, passing everyone and dropping the research paper from your future course plans.

3. Developing a series of separate exercises on research skills such as finding secondary sources and footnoting to supplement the text and, in the future, using them in place of an actual paper.

4. Reviewing certain typical papers in class to show the students their faults.

5. Requiring your students to hand in several stages of preliminary drafts which outline and preview their purpose, references, and main ideas according to a strict schedule that allows you to monitor their progress.

Now, What Would You Do About the Research Paper?

Explain Why You Would Do That

One More Thing To Do

Examine the following:

> Ken Macrorie. "I-Searching," *Searching Writing* (Boynton/Cook, 1980), pp. 53-197.

CASE 28

Choosing Things for Other People to Read

"This is the most boring thing I've ever read!"

"Why do we have to read this dumb story?"

"I don't care about them. They aren't anything like me. Why can't we read about people like us?"

With these comments ringing in your ears, your first literature unit drew to its close. You had realized as the days passed that the students did not seem to like what they were being asked to read. Their "evaluations" confirmed your fears but didn't help you much in correcting the problem. Your classes are not unwilling to discuss the people, problems, and ideas they find in the works they read; they just don't seem to like what you select.

As you think about it, the problem seems to be twofold. First, there are some students who just cannot understand the reading, either because they are poor readers or because they are too immature for the works.

Second, a larger group understands but is not interested in what you have assigned. Obviously, it is difficult to select works for people like Mary, who is shy, romantic, very religious, and rather prudish; Joe, whose only interests are cars and sports; and George, who, to be tactful, already is leading a very adult life.

Still, they are all teenagers and seem to have a lot in common. At least, they seem to understand and be able to talk to each other a lot better than they can to adults such as you and their parents.

You wonder what works of literature at least a majority of them will like.

A Few Questions You Might Ask Yourself

1. What kinds of things are adolescents interested in reading about? What kind of book would appeal to Mary? To Joe? To George?

2. What kinds of classroom activities might help ensure a high level of student interest? What kinds of books would lend themselves to such activities?

3. How do students respond to books like *To Kill a Mockingbird*, *The Chocolate War*, and *A Day No Pigs Would Die*? To what extent should you be selecting young adult novels, that is, novels in modern idiom about and written for modern adolescents?

Some Things For You To Do Next

1. Examine the required novels listed in the curriculum of a local school. Consider which you think will be the most appealing. The least appealing.

2.   Read

     Robert Small. "Some of My Favorite Books Are by Young Adult Authors
     and Some Are by Jane Austen," *English Journal*, April, 1986, pp. 81-84.

3.   Read several recent, popular novels written for teenagers selected from those
     Small mentions and consider which of these merit study by whole classes.

4.   Discuss with a high school librarian the books that students check out most
     often. Examine the most popular and consider their characteristics:
     vocabulary, sentence structure, literary complexity, subjects.

What Do You Think Of Doing The Following?

1.   Replacing the classics you had planned to teach with simplified and
     modernized versions.

2.   Planning for several groups of students with common interests to read works
     which correspond to those interests.

3.   Sticking with the classics in the text on the theory that students don't have to
     like everything they read and should be instructed in a common literary
     heritage.

4. Giving the students brief descriptions of a number of books that might appeal to them (perhaps from a school book club's monthly offering) and letting them select a book for the class to read and study.

Now, Select A Work Of Young Adult Literature That You Believe Teenagers Would Enjoy Studying Together And Describe How You Would Teach It

Explain Why You Selected That Work And Why You Would Teach It In The Way You Described

One More Thing You Might Do

Read the following article that opposes using young adult literature:

Frank G. Jennings. "Literature for Adolescents -- Pap or Protein?" in
Richard A. Meade and Robert C. Small, Jr., eds., *Literature for
Adolescents: Selection and Use* (Charles E. Merrill, 1973), pp.
95-102.

The Uninspired
Papers

So far this year, you have asked your average tenth-grade class to write three compositions. Carefully avoiding the trite -- "What I Did During My Summer Vacation" -- and the very abstract -- "Justice" -- you have sought out topics which seem to relate to your students' lives. You've also given them choices of topics; and, in desperation, for the last assignment, you gave them complete freedom to choose their own topics. Although most of the students have written the required papers, the results have been, with one or two exceptions, poorly written, shallow, and dull.

On your first assignment -- "Changing Our Town to Make It Liveable" -- Jane, Tom, and one or two other students wrote rather well. The rest of the students pointed with remarkably little enthusiasm about obvious improvements such as a public swimming pool and better parking downtown. On the second paper -- "Your Pet Dislike" -- Jane wrote well again, her pet dislike being dull English composition assignments. Jack, a second stringer on the football team, did fairly well in attacking the head football coach. The rest of the papers were uninteresting, unimpassioned examples of fulfilling assignments. No feeling of dislike came through.

Agitated, you made your next assignment a "free" theme -- "Write About Whatever You Want to Write About" -- hoping that you would release a flood of pent-up ideas. The assignment was even less successful than the earlier two. With nothing left to attack, even Jane turned in a drab piece of work. Not only were the papers growing duller, they showed no improvement in organization, mechanics, and so forth despite your diligent marking.

From discussions with the students, you have finally concluded that the problem is a result of a lack of interest by most of them in writing about a particular topic at a particular time. Yet the free theme was also a disaster. Clearly they see no purpose in writing your assignments other than to receive a passing grade. And so they wait until the night before the assignment is due and hurriedly write something to turn in. How, you ask yourself, can I get them interested in writing? What can I do before they start to write to give them a real sense of purpose?

A Few Questions You Might Ask Yourself

1. Why do people write outside a school setting? When do they choose to write something? Why?

2. When would you feel a strong urge to sit down and write about something? What would cause you to have that feeling?

3. What kinds of readers do most people write for? What kinds of readers are assignments in English class usually done for? Is the difference important?

4.   What kinds of subjects, problems, etc. are of most interest to teenagers? How can a teacher turn those interests into topics which students will want to write about?

5.   How do successful writers go about writing? When you write something from choice, do you have any usual way of doing the writing?

6.   What kinds of prewriting exercises involving talking, acting, and writing can you assign to warm-up your dull writers?

7.   What kind of revision assignments might enliven your students' writing?

Some Things For You To Do Next

1.   Read the following:

John H. Bushman. Ch. 1: "Teaching Writing: An Overview" and Ch. 2: "Classroom Climate and the Teaching of Writing," in *The Teaching of Writing* (Charles C. Thomas, 1984), pp. 3-37.

2.   Review the rhetorical concepts of invention, audience, tone, purpose, occasion, mode, persona, voice, and style. Consider how you can apply these concepts in your lessons on composition.

What Do You Think Of Doing The Following?

1.   Assigning the students several short stories to read, discussing them in class, and using the most successful discussion as a basis for the next paper.

2. Explaining to the class that in college and in business, people have to write constantly on subjects they are not interested in and that success is dependent on doing a good job anyway.

3. Collecting examples of lively and effective writing to serve as models for your students.

4. Collecting the first drafts of the students' papers and showing them where they can make their papers more interesting.

5. Requiring your students to keep a weekly journal of observations, feelings, and ideas that can serve as material for their papers.

6. Inviting in local newspaper columnists noted for their wit to share their secrets of lively writing with your students.

Now, Explain What You Would Do To Combat Lack Of Interest In Writing

Explain Why You Would Do That

One More Thing You Might Do

Read

Joseph Strzepek. "How Do You Talk to a Tiger?" *Virginia English Bulletin*, Spring, 1979, pp. 10-14.

an article dramatizing the importance of audience, occasion, and persona in writing.

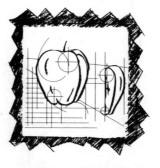

Dealing with the Dictionary

As part of the eighth-grade English curriculum, your students are, as the curriculum guide states, supposed to "develop skill in the use of the dictionary, understanding of the nature of the dictionary, and a positive attitude toward the dictionary as a valuable tool and for an educated person." Although you might have worded the goals differently, they seem worthwhile.

However, when you look into the chapter on the use of the dictionary in the grammar-composition book, somehow you can't see your students benefitting from the text and the exercises. A number of pages are devoted to alphabetizing, the abbreviations and symbols used in dictionaries, headwords, synonyms and antonyms, pronunciation keys, prefixes and suffixes, and other such matters. Most of the exercises do require that the students actually use a dictionary, but most of them also strike you as dry and mechanical.

When you ask several other English teachers in the school what they do, you discover that they feel that dictionary lessons are bound to be dull and, though none of them put it that way, are only meant to develop low-level, mechanical skills, despite the high-sounding language of the objective in the curriculum guide. Three of your colleagues explain that they follow the grammar-composition text exactly. Two others admit to skipping that part of the curriculum.

"It's funny," Barbara Preston says with a wink, "but I just never seem to have time to get to that. June always comes first."

Sarah Simpson tells you that she teaches the dictionary "functionally." As far as you can determine, "functionally" means that the students are expected to use the dictionary now and then and to find correct spellings and meanings.

To see how much your students already know about the use of a dictionary, you give out a set of dictionaries and ask the class to find the answers to a list of questions designed to test a person's skill in and general understanding of dictionaries. Most of the students do poorly, and the exercise takes all of them far longer to complete than you expected. In addition, they quickly become bored and restless with what they clearly see as useless busy work. It is obvious that they do not have the skill and understanding asked for in the curriculum guide; the boredom with which they face the task makes you doubt their "positive attitude"; and you know that they avoid using it even to find spelling and meanings.

Yet you remember an essay you read in a linguistics book in college that dealt with the way a dictionary is produced and the difficult decisions that lexicographers have to make. In fact, you still enjoy looking through dictionaries and reading a definition and word history now and then. Whenever you look up one word, you always find yourself reading about the words that are listed on the same page with that word. You feel sure that there is more to dictionaries than alphabetizing exercises and that there must be ways to develop both the skills needed for using and an interest in dictionaries.

A Few Questions You Might Ask Yourself

1. How often do you use a dictionary? For what do you use it? How skillful are you in using it?

2. On what occasions would students need to use a dictionary? What problems might they face? Why do you think they avoid using it?

3. Is it possible for a person actually to like dictionaries? What is your own feeling about them? What might be interesting about a dictionary aside from its practical value as a source of information?

4. How many different kinds of dictionaries are you familiar with?

5. How might students develop skill in the use of a dictionary without being bored by it?

Some Things For You To Do Next

1. Examine the dictionary lessons in a standard grammar-composition book and consider the nature of the explanatory material and the exercises.

2. Examine *Webster's Collegiate Dictionary* and the *American Heritage Dictionary*. Look up some words and study the various kinds of information available. Examine the other kinds of information such as maps and biographical sketches that they contain.

3. Read the following:

   Don F. Jones, "The Dictionary: A Look at 'Look It Up'," *Journal of Reading*, January, 1980, pp. 309-312.

4. Discuss dictionaries with some of your non-English-major friends. Try to discover how they feel about the dictionary, what they know about it, and how and why they make use of it.

5. Explore the collection of your school library to see how many different kinds of dictionaries you can find.

What Do You Think Of Doing The Following?

1. Concentrating your lessons on the skills needed to use a dictionary quickly and accurately but spreading the lessons out over the entire year by establishing a dictionary day each week.

2. Accepting the "functional" approach and trying to make it work by creating opportunities for students to use the dictionary in connection with other work.

3. Mounting a campaign to get all subject areas within the school to emphasize the dictionary as a valuable tool.

4. Developing a lecture on the history of the dictionary.

5. Having the major project of your dictionary unit require each student to develop a dictionary of words related to a special recreational or vocational interest.

Now, How Would You Teach The Dictionary?

Explain Why You Would Do That

One More Thing You Might Do

Read the following:

Robert Small. "Junior Lexicographers," *Ideas Plus* (NCTE, 1985), pp. 3-4.

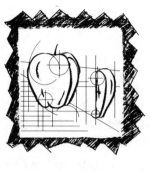

The Spoken or Mumbled Word

"And, uh, then, well, I think maybe, uh, he meant, uh, you know, . . ."

A not unintelligent student, John probably has a worthwhile idea to contribute to the class discussion, yet you know by this time that he will stammer his way to total incoherence and confusion. You will then have to try to make sense of what he has said or call on someone else. John is not the only student with this problem. In fact, many of the students in this average ninth-grade class seem, despite their writing problems, to be better at expressing themselves in writing than in speech.

At times you have tried to help them by suggesting expressions they seem to be groping for, but usually they merely let you have the floor and retire to silence. Criticism almost always makes the incoherent worse. In the grammar-composition book that your school uses, there is a chapter on speaking, with sections on public speaking, debate, and discussion. You seriously consider using it; but, in fact, you feel that the problem is not so much inability to handle formal speaking situations as a more fundamental incapacity to put ideas quickly into words. Although many of your students would no doubt have difficulty preparing and delivering a formal speech, others who write well could probably memorize a speech.

You wonder if they would articulate more clearly if they had prepared comments.

You are pretty sure that George, Jack, and several others have ideas and would express them if they didn't find talking awkward. How can you help your students to talk naturally and clearly? Would a unit in public speaking help take care of the problem? Or would practice in dramatic improvisation be more useful?

A Few Questions You Might Ask Yourself

1. How smoothly do most people talk when in a discussion? What factors might influence the smoothness: preparation, confidence, the supportive or competitive atmosphere of the class?

2. When do you think students would have the most difficulty expressing themselves in class?

3. What are the primary similarities and differences between formal public speaking and less formal discussion and conversation? What are the differences between recitations, debates, and discussions? Between large and small-group discussions?

4. How does a person learn to put his/her thoughts quickly into words? What skills are involved? What kind of practice will develop those skills?

5. Do teachers do anything to inhibit articulate responses by the ways to ask and pace questions and respond to their responses?

Some Things For You To Do Next

1. Listen to a discussion among a number of friends, and consider their ease of expression.

2. Examine the chapters on speaking in a standard high school grammar-composition text and consider the relationship of the material there to the general problems students have in oral self-expression.

3. Compare discussions that are preceded by such warm-up activities as writing assignments to discussions which you jump into directly.

4. In *Active Voice* (Boyton/Cook, 1981), James Moffett says we should have students write dialogue before asking them to hold forth in monologues. Consider whether or not asking students to write dialogues between characters in literature and reading those dialogues to each other in small groups before discussing them in a large group would help with the problem.

What Do You Think Of Doing The Following?

1. Teaching the public speaking unit in the textbook and assuming that the practice will do the students good.

2. Calling on those students who have oral problems in order to make sure that they have a chance to develop their skills.

3. Using considerable small-group work on the assumption that students will feel more comfortable expressing themselves in such a setting than in a large class.

4. Assigning oral reports, panel discussions, debates, etc. as a means of conducting the work of the class and at the same time providing opportunities for work on oral expression.

5. Inviting the school drama teacher to lead your class through a series of activities designed to reduce anxiety before oral performances.

Now, What Would You Do To Improve Speaking Skills?

Explain Why You Would Do That

One More Thing You Might Do

Read the following:

> B. D. Stanford. "Fostering Practical Communication Skills," *English Journal*, October, 1970, pp. 967-969.

CASE 32

Playing Games

Recently you have been hearing a good deal of talk about such things as role-playing and simulation games as ways to make learning real and alive for students. The social studies teachers in your school seem to be using war games, games of politics, and games dealing with social problems in nearly every class.

Helen Bradford said in the teachers' lounge just the other day, "I don't know how I ever taught that world geography class without that game about establishing a city. It makes all the difference, I can tell you."

And at the last PTA meeting, Rick Madison and Joy Barnes, two biology teachers, demonstrated several games that they had been using. They did an excellent job of showing why the games were effective teaching devices. The parents seemed to be impressed, although one mother was heard to say something about not sending her son to high school to play games.

All your colleagues in science and social studies seem to agree that simulation games and role-playing help a lot to teach students an understanding of such areas as the political system, environmental problems, and social systems.

In your own classes, you have occasionally used spelling games and crossword puzzles; and, once or twice, as a review, you have used games based on television quiz shows. But you really aren't satisfied that you are making the fullest and best use of games. Somehow, you feel sure that role-playing and other kinds of learning games ought to be especially effective teaching devices, particularly for composition and literature study.

You've been looking through the materials catalogues that are kept in the library; but, under the heading "Language Arts," you haven't found what you've been looking for. All the games shown for English in those catalogues have been the same low-level word games that are not much more than glorified drills, especially those played on a computer. You've taken a look at the social studies and science games, but they just don't seem to apply very well to English. Helen offered to let you use the city building games, and you've been toying with the idea of trying to use it to introduce a composition assignment.

Still, there ought to be lots of simulation games and role-playing games for English. Could I invent one, you've wondered. The science and social studies ones seem simple enough; but, of course, you've seen them only after someone else has worked out all the problems. You're pretty sure that making one is harder than it seems. And when you tried making up a simulation game to prepare the students for *The Pearl*, you discovered that you had overlooked so many details in the planning that it didn't work at all, although the students went along with it without much complaining.

Still, you're back where you started, wondering whether or not there really is a place for games in the English program.

A Few Questions You Might Ask Yourself

1. What advantages can you think of for the use of games in teaching? Is the fact that students like them the principal one?

2. What parts of the English program might lend themselves best to the use of games?

3. What are the characteristics of games? Do they in fact lend themselves to science and social studies better than to English? Why?

4. How can playing games improve reading and thinking skills?

Some Things For You To Do Next

1. Examine several games designed for science and for social studies classes and consider how they are planned. Ask yourself what they teach and how.

2. Read the following:

    John Hollowell and Kenneth Davis. "Why Play Games?" (pp. 1-7) and Irvin Hashimoto, "Why *Not* to Play Games" (pp. 37-42), in K. Davis and J. Hollowell, eds. *Inventing and Playing Games in the English Classroom* (NCTE, 1977).

3. Examine some of the many word games, puzzles, etc. and consider how useful they are and how they are different from the social studies and science games you examined.

4. Review the logical puzzles in Ken Weber's *Yes, They Can* (Metheun, 1974).

5. Review samples from the analytical and verbal sections in the college board exam and consider what English teachers can do to help students win those "games."

6. Review at least two computerized language arts or English games.

What Do You Think Of Doing The Following?

1. Borrowing an environment game from the social studies department and using it to introduce a work of literature, such as *The Wave* by Morton Rhue, that deals with social problems.

2. Deciding to stick to word games and puzzles because English just doesn't lend itself to learning through simulation games.

3. Using role playing extensively to explore literature, to stimulate composition, and to examine dialects and other aspects of language but not as a part of formal games.

4. Deciding to spend next summer developing several situation games to use with your classes.

5. Rejecting all games as soft education.

Now, Describe How You Might Use Games In English

Explain Why You Would Use Games In Those Ways

One More Thing You Might Do

Read the following:

Mike Beary, Gary Saloner, and Robert Wesolowski. "How to Run the
Game" (pp. 8-19) and John Hollowell, "How to Design the
Game" (pp. 20-28), in K. Davis and J. Hollowell, eds., *Inventing
and Playing Games in the English Classroom* (NCTE, 1977).

Then examine several of the games described in the second part of the Davis and
Hollowell book.

The Unplanned Lesson

It seemed like a good idea when it occurred to you. You were driving to school on that rainy Tuesday and worrying about your second-period class. The students just didn't seem to be grasping the question of authority in *Lord of the Flies*. They especially had failed to understand the inability of the right and wise to exert authority unsupported by some greater power.

Then, sitting waiting for a traffic light to change and watching the windshield wipers move back and forth, you had the idea to stage a situation in your class from which a conflict could arise. You'd considered staging a conflict between you and another teacher but decided that a conflict between you and a student would work better so that you could use the results to promote a discussion of a teacher's authority and what backs it up. Then you could go on to authority in general and *Lord of the Flies* in particular.

Like so many of your good ideas, however, this one failed miserably. John was the boy you picked to argue with you as the students came into class. You told him to challenge your authority, to refuse to do something you'd told him to do. There wasn't much time to explain before class started.

When the time came, he couldn't think of anything to say. So he just stammered something about, "You can't make me do that," without anyone knowing what it was you were trying to make him do or why he wouldn't do it. And the class never believed that he was really causing trouble since he was just about the meekest kid in class and had never misbehaved before. That was why you chose him, of course. He was safe.

Then you weren't sure what to do next. You started to send John to the Principal's Office, then hesitated because John wouldn't have any place to go while the class discussed what had happened. Then you sent him anyway.

Finally, you realized that you didn't have any smooth way to move from the staged incident to a class discussion of it without sacrificing the supposed reality of it. Since teachers rarely discuss individual discipline problems with entire classes, you didn't think you could say casually, "Let's discuss what just happened." If the students weren't already suspicious, doing that would surely give your strategy away.

And, while you were trying to figure out how to save the situation, John stuck his head in the door and asked whether he could come back in now. That was the final blow. The whole class laughed; and, blushing a bit, you had to laugh too. What a disaster!

As you thought about it later, you realized that much the same kind of thing seemed to happen every time you tried some activity more imaginative than "going over" the textbook or checking homework. You think you have good ideas. They seem to be as good as most that you read about in the *English Journal*. But they rarely work.

A Few Questions You Might Ask Yourself

1. In what specific ways did the class not work? How many of the problems which arose could you have anticipated? How many of them could you have avoided?

2. Was the idea really a good one, or does the fact that it produced so many problems mean it was a poor idea?

3. How might you have laid out a plan for this activity so that its success was ensured?

4. How much preparation does a teacher have to do? What does preparation entail? Are there different kinds of preparation? Do they involve different kinds of skills?

Some Things For You To Do Next

1. Read pages 33 through 43 in T. W. Hipple's *Teaching English in Secondary Schools* (Macmillan, 1973), then

    Read the following:
    Raymond J. Rodrigues and Dennis Bodoczewski. *A Guide Book for Teaching Literature*, pp. 189-213 (Allyn & Bacon, 1978).

2. Interview several teachers. Ask them questions dealing with the kinds and amount of planning they do. Observe several teachers and try to determine how much planning went into the lessons. Can you determine if there is a relation between planning and the success of a class?

3. Using several friends as a class, choose a teaching idea from E. J. Farrell's "Listen, My Children, and You Shall Read," *English Journal*, January, 1966, pp. 39-45, 68, and attempt to carry it out without planning how to do it. Consider what aspects would have worked better if you had given them more careful thought.

What Do You Think Of Doing The Following?

1. Deciding that you just cannot handle complicated activities and concentrating on the type of teaching you do seem to be able to do.

2. Looking for activities that are described in detail in articles, books, and teaching guides and following the plans closely.

3. Relying on experience to take care of the problem.

4. Writing out in advance a detailed "script" for each class period and following it exactly.

5. Submitting your plans to one or more fellow teachers for advice and criticism.

Now, Write A Plan For The Activity Described In The Case

Explain Why You Planned That Way

One More Thing You Might Do

Take the same idea from Farrell's article that you tried to teach without plans, and develop a complete set of plans for it.

Bibliography

"A Proposed Position Statement: Students' Right to Their Own Language, *Conference on College Composition and Communication*, Spring 1974, pp. 1-19.

Anderson, Richard C., et al. *Becoming a Nation of Readers*. National Academy of Education, 1984.

Beary, Mike, Gary Salvner, and Robert Wesolowski. "How to Run the Game," in K. Davis and J. Holloway, eds. *Inventing and Playing Games in the English Classroom*. NCTE, 1977, pp. 8-19.

Booth, Wayne. "Censorship and the Values of Fiction," *English Journal*, March, 1964, pp. 155-164.

Bushman, John H. *The Teaching of Writing*. Charles C. Thomas, 1984.

Bushman, John H. and Kay Parks Bushman. *Teaching English Creatively*. Charles C. Thomas, 1986.

Chapman, Abraham, ed. *Black Voices*. New American Library, 1968.

Christenberry, Leila and Patricia Kelly. *Questioning: A Path to Critical Thinking*. NCTE, 1983.

Crapse, Larry. "A Symposium on Pre-1900 Classics Worth Teaching," *English Journal*, March, 1983, pp. 51-52.

Crews, Frederick. *Pooh Perplex: A Freshman Casebook*. Dutton, 1965.

Dant, Doris R. "Plagarism in High School: A Survey," *English Journal*, February, 1986, pp. 81-84.

Davis, Kenneth and John Hollowell, eds. *Inventing and Playing Games in the English Classroom*. NCTE, 1977.

Duke, Charles R. and Jacobsen, Sally A. eds., *Reading and Writing Poetry: Successful Approaches for the Student and Teacher*. Oryx Press, 1983.

Elbow, Peter. *Writing with Power*. Oxford University Press, 1981.

Estes, Thomas H. and Joseph L. Vaughn. *Reading and Learning in the Classroom*. Allyn & Bacon, 1985.

Fader, Daniel, et al. *The New Hooked on Books.* Berkley, 1976.

Farrell, E. J. "Listen My Children, and You Shall Read," *English Journal*, January, 1966, pp. 39-45; 68.

Gallo, Donald, ed. *Books for You.* NCTE, 1986.

Hashimoto, Irvin. "Why *Not* to Play Games," in Kenneth Davis and John Hollowell, eds. *Inventing and Playing Games in the English Classroom.* NCTE, 1977, pp. 37-42.

Hayakawa, S. I. *Language in Thought and Action.* Harcourt Brace Jovanovich, 1972.

Hipple, T. W. *Teaching English in Secondary Schools.* Macmillan, 1973.

Hodges, Richard E. *Improving Spelling and Vocabulary in the Secondary School.* NCTE, 1982.

Hoetker, James. *Students as Audience: An Experimental Study of the Relationships between Classroom Study of Drama and Attendance at the Theater.* NCTE Research Report No. 11. NCTE, 1971.

Hopkins, Lee Bennett. *Moments.* Harcourt Brace Jovanovich, 1980.

Hollowell, John. "How to Design the Game," in Kenneth Davis and John Hollowell, eds. *Inventing and Playing Games in the English Classroom.* NCTE, 1977, pp. 20-28.

Hollowell, John and Kenneth Davis. "Why Play Games?" in Kenneth Davis and John Hollowell, eds. *Inventing and Playing Games in the English Classroom*. NCTE, 1977, pp. 1-7.

Hunt, Lyman C., Jr. "Six Steps to the Individualized Reading Program (IRP)," *Elementary English*, January, 1971, pp. 22-32.

Jenkinson, Edward. "Protecting Holden Caulfield and His Friends from the Censors," *English Journal*, January, 1985, pp. 26-33.

Jennings, Frank S. "Literature for Adolescents: Pap or Protein?" in Richard A. Meade and Robert Small, eds. *Literature for Adolescents: Selection and Use*. Charles E. Merrill, 1973.

Jones, Don F. "The Dictionary: A Look at Look It Up," *Journal of Reading*, January, 1980, pp. 309-312.

Jones, Michael. "The Making of a Poetry Program," *English Journal*, October, 1985, pp. 63-65.

Kaufman, Bella. *Up the Down Staircase*. Prentice-Hall, 1964.

Kelly, Patricia, Mary Pat Hall, and Robert Small. "Composition through the Team Approach," *English Journal*, September, 1984, pp. 71-74.

Kirby, Dan and Tom Liner. *Inside Out*. Boynton/Cook, 1981.

Kirby, Dan and Carol Kuykendall. *Thinking Through Language: Book One*. NCTE, 1985.

Koch, Kenneth. *Rose, Where Did You Get That Red?* Random House, 1973.

Laird, Charlton. "Down Gaintwife: The Uses of Etymology," *English Journal*, November, 1970, pp. 1106-1112.

Macrorie, Kenneth. "To Be Read," in Richard L. Graves, ed. *Rhetoric and Composition*. Hayden Book Company, 1984, pp. 81-88.

Macrorie, Kenneth. *Searching Writing*. Boynton/Cook, 1980.

Macrorie, Kenneth. *Writing To Be Read*. Boynton/Cook, 1976.

Mawdsley, Ralph D. *Legal Aspects of Plagiarism*. National Organization on Legal Problems in Education, 1985.

Moffett, James. *Active Voice*. Boynton/Cook, 1981.

Moffett, James. *Teaching the Universe of Discourse*. Houghton Mifflin, 1983.

Moffett, James. *A Student-Centered Language Arts Curriculum, K-12*. Houghton Mifflin, 1968.

O'Hare, Frank, *Sentence Combining: Improving Student Writing Without Formal Grammar Instruction*, Research Report No. 15. NCTE, 1973.

Probst, Robert E. *Adolescent Literature: Response and Analysis*. Charles E. Merrill, 1984.

Purvis, Alan. "Evaluation of Learning" in Benjamin Bloom, ed. *Handbook on Summative and Formative Evaluation of Student Learning*. McGraw-Hill, 1971, pp. 697-766.

Reed, Arthea J. S. *Reaching Adolescents: The Young Adult Book and the School.* Holt, Rinehart and Winston, 1985.

Rodrigues, Raymond and Dennis Bododzewski. *A Guide for Teaching Literature.* Allyn & Bacon, 1978.

Shaftel, Fannie R. and George Shaftel. *Role Playing for Social Values.* Prentice-Hall, 1967.

Shawnessy, Mina. *Errors and Expectations.* Oxford University Press, 1977.

Simmon, Susan. "Pip -- a Love Affair," *English Journal*, March, 1969, pp. 416-417.

Simonini, R. C., Jr. "Word Making in Present Day English," *English Journal*, September, 1966, pp. 752-757.

Sledd, James. "Bidialectism: The Linguistics of White Supremacy," *English Journal*, December, 1969, pp. 1307-1315; 1329.

Small, Robert. "Junior Lexicographers," *Ideas Plus*, NCTE, 1985, pp. 3-4.

Small, Robert. "Some of My Favorite Books Are by Young Adult Authors and Some Are by Jane Austen," *English Journal*, April, 1986, pp. 81-84.

Stanford, Barbara Dodds. "Fostering Practical Communication Skills," *English Journal*, October, 1970, pp. 967-969.

Stanford, Barbara Dodds and Karima Amin. *Black Literature for High School Students.* NCTE, 1978.

Stanford, Barbara and Gene Stanford. *Thinking Through Language: Book Two.* NCTE, 1985.

Stanford, Gene, ed. "Getting Involved in Poetry," *Activating the Passive Student*, 1979, pp. 95-121.

Stillman, Peter. *Writing Your Way.* Boynton/Cook, 1984.

Strickland, Dorothy S. *Listen Children: An Anthology of Black Literature.* Bantam, 1982.

Strong, William. *Practing Sentence Options.* Random House, 1984.

Strzepek, Joseph. "How Do You Talk to a Tiger?" *Virginia English Bulletin*, Spring 1979, pp. 10-14.

Weber, Ken. *Yes, They Can.* Metheun, 1974.

West, William W. *Teaching the Gifted and Talented in the English Classroom.* National Education Association, 1980.

Wolfe, Denny. *Making the Grade: Evaluating and Judging Student Writing.* Coronado, 1986.

Workman, Brooke. *Writing Seminars in the Content Area: In Search of Hemingway, Salinger, and Steinbeck.* NCTE, 1983.

Topical Index